# ASSESSING MEDIA EDUCATION

# LEA'S COMMUNICATION SERIES
## Jennings Bryant / Dolf Zillmann, General Editors

For a complete list of titles in LEA's Communication Series, please contact Lawrence Erlbaum Associates, Publishers at www.erlbaum.com

# ASSESSING MEDIA EDUCATION

## A Resource Handbook
## for Educators and Administrators

## COMPONENT 1: MEASUREMENT

*Edited by*

**William G. Christ**
*Trinity University*

LAWRENCE ERLBAUM ASSOCIATES, PUBLISHERS
2007   Mahwah, New Jersey                    London

KH

This volume is an abridged version of *Assessing Media Education: A Resource Handbook for Educators and Administrators*, edited by William G. Christ. Additional components and the complete volume are available from Lawrence Erlbaum Associates, Inc. at www.erlbaum.com.

Lawrence Erlbaum Associates, Inc., Publishers
10 Industrial Avenue
Mahwah, New Jersey 07430
www.erlbaum.com

Cover design by Kathryn Houghtaling

**Library of Congress Cataloging-in-Publication DataP**

Assessing media education : a resource handbook for educators and administrators / edited by William G. Christ.
    p. cm.
Includes bibliographical references and index.
ISBN 0-8058-6092-4 (pbk. : alk. paper)
1. Mass media—Study and teaching (Higher)—Evaluation—Handbooks, manuals, etc. I. Christ, William G.
P91.3.A853 2005
302.23'071'1—dc22                      2005051015
                                              CIP

Printed in the United States of America
10  9  8  7  6  5  4  3  2  1

10/19/06

# Contents

# Preface

Assessment is an integral part of what we do as teachers, researchers, and administrators. It can be formal or informal, systematic or haphazard, harmful or rewarding. At its best, assessment can have a transforming effect on education. At its worst, it can be used as an instrument to punish people and programs.

We are living in the age of accountability. Though calls for accountability and assessment have come and gone, the current demands for proving that students are learning seem more insistent as they become codified in educational policies. The move from asking teachers what they teach to requiring programs to show that students are learning is a paradigm shift that costs blood, sweat, and tears. It requires educators to look differently at their curricula, courses, syllabuses, and measurement mechanisms.

The purpose of this book is to provide useful information to those in higher education media programs who want to create or improve their student learning assessment strategies. This component, Part III, in the main volume, systematically presents both indirect and direct measures of student learning outcomes from advisory boards to examinations.

If assessment is here to stay, then it is important for media educators to understand and use the process so that they control their own destinies. The hope is that this book will be a useful intellectual and practical resource for media educators and administrators as they grapple with the challenges of assessment.

## ACKNOWLEDGMENTS

This book has been a very rewarding collaboration. I would like to publicly acknowledge the hard work of the authors involved in this project. Working with these authors has been a true pleasure. Their care and expertise will be evident to you as you read each chapter.

Second, I would like to thank the people at Lawrence Erlbaum Associates. Linda Bathgate was a major force behind the conceptualization and execution of this book. Nadine Simms has done a great job keeping the production side of the book on track. Tina Hardy did an excellent job as copy editor. The anonymous critiques of the early prospectus by conscientious reviewers made this a stronger book. I appreciate all their hard work.

From Trinity University, I would like to thank my department and the administration for their support. Trinity is an intellectually stimulating place where educational issues dealing with teaching, courses, and curricula are vigorously debated.

On a more personal note, I would like to thank those who developed the Internet and email. This project would have taken twice as long without these new communication technologies. I would also like to thank my sons Nathan and Jonathan Christ and especially my life partner, wife, and true friend, Judith Anne Christ.

Thank you one and all.

—*William G. Christ*
*San Antonio, Texas*

# Component 1
# Assessing Media Education
# Measuring Student Learning Outcomes

## Introduction to Component 1

The chapters in this book are part of a larger book titled *Assessing Media Education: A Resource Handbook for Educators and Administrators*. This component will be useful for those educators who have already developed an assessment plan and identified key student learning outcomes, and who now need information on how to measure the outcomes, both indirectly and directly.

# Introduction:
# Why Assessment Matters[1]

William G. Christ
*Department of Communication*
*Trinity University*

> *Accountability to my students meant: plan the course, show up in class, keep it moving, comment thoughtfully on papers, mentor when asked, submit grades, write recommendations—the usual packet of services. My obligation to my departmental colleagues: take on my share of core courses and administrative duties. To administrators and trustees: just don't make scenes, I guess; the thought rarely crossed my mind. My responsibility to society as a whole: I cheerfully held myself accountable for the wretched of the earth. . . .*
>
> —Ohmann (2000, p. 24)

If the programmatic assessment of student learning outcomes was universally acknowledged as being necessary, important, and positive, then it would not need to be defended. Yet, even those who accept the assessment of student learning outcomes in principle can find the job of planning, assessing, tabulating, and reporting so cumbersome and costly that they feel anger toward assessment efforts.

The assessment of student learning outcomes has become the acid test for media educators. It requires a paradigm shift in a faculty's thinking. Instead of focusing on traditional assessment "inputs" like faculty degrees, number of full-time faculty, research productivity, resources, facilities, equipment, diversity, and curriculum, a student learning ap-

---

[1]An earlier version of this chapter was in the Association of Schools of Journalism and Mass Communication *Insights* periodical.

proach to assessment focuses on "outputs." Instead of asking "what do faculty need to teach," the question becomes "what do we want students to learn?" "The question, 'What is basic about our discipline?' becomes 'What is basic about the discipline that students should learn and how do we know they have learned it?' " (Christ, McCall, Rakow, & Blanchard, 1997, p. 29).

Simply stated, faculty do assessment for either internal or external reasons. Yet, where we are in the assessment debates only makes sense within the broader context of off-campus forces impacting campuses. The first part of this chapter, therefore, outlines off-campus forces. Then, definitions are given and the two reasons are laid out.

## OFF-CAMPUS FORCES

Jones, Jones, and Hargrove (2003) wrote that the first documented achievement tests can be linked to the mid-1800s when "the United States began an unprecedented effort to educate the masses" (p. 14). Janesick (2001, p. 89), who made a distinction between the testing movement (just after World War I) and the assessment movement, suggested that researchers should go back to the 1880s, "when Francis Galton, in London, administered tests to hundreds of persons to test sensory reactions and reaction times of volunteers," to understand the "big picture" of assessment. Both authors document the growth of public education after World War II and the transformative nature of the 1960s. Whereas Janesick argued that Howard Gardner's research on his theory of multiple intelligences almost "single-handedly starts the assessment movement" (p. 92), both researchers indicate the importance of the 1983 United States Department of Education's National Commission on Excellence in Education publication, "A Nation at Risk: The Imperative for Educational Reform" (1983), that "clearly situated public education as being in crisis and in need of major reform. The report used test scores as the indicator of success and the goal of schooling" (Jones et al., 2003, p. 15). The use of test scores as valid measures of excellence can be seen in the use of standardized tests like the Scholastic Assessment Test, American College Testing, and the Graduate Record Exam, and in the highly politicized "No Child Left Behind Act of 2001" (2002) legislation.

### The Accountability Movement

Assessment is part of a larger accountability movement. Although it is clear from the previous discussion that accountability concerns are not new (see also Martin, Overholt, & Urban, 1976, pp. 33–41), Ohmann

(2000) has suggested that the current accountability movement grew out of three main forces in the late 1960s and early 1970s. The first "was an intense fiscal crisis of the state, brought on partly by war spending, but expressed chiefly as disillusionment with Great Society programs" (p. 28). Educational costs and expenditures had increased during the 1960s and there was concern that, as then deputy commissioner in the Office of Education Terrel H. Bell reported, "Money alone could not buy good education . . ." (p. 28).

Second, Ohmann (2000) argued that the accountability movement "was partly a counterthrust against liberatory ideas and experiments in 'open education,' that is, against the critique of schooling mounted by sixties visionaries and radicals" (p. 28). If the 1960s stood for student power, a democratization of higher education, and challenges to the educational status quo, then the rise of accountability in education could be seen as a direct challenge to these forces, suggesting to some that "traditional notions about the value of democracy and the value of the individual are ultimately at stake" (Martin et al., 1976, p. 6).

Finally, the third main force driving the accountability movement in education was a reaction against the "turmoil and disruption on the campuses; political action by students and faculty members . . . ; and mounting distrust of higher education by the public . . ." (Ohmann, 2000, p. 28). This led to "the increasing demand for colleges and universities to justify what they are doing and to disclose the effectiveness and efficiency of their operations" (McConnell, 1972, p. 200). Seen in this light, "one explanation for the failure of accountability advocates to heed objections by educators is that accountability is not primarily a pedagogical movement. It is an administrative system, and as such it is impervious to arguments which are based on educational concerns" (Martin et al., 1976, p. 32).

As the modern day accountability movement was building steam in the mid-1970s, there were a number of educators who wrote scathing critiques. Martin et al. (1976), in their critique of accountability in higher education, identified three major defects: "First, it lacks an adequate theoretical base" (p. 6). Accountability is a complex construct that is not always fully investigated and explicated by those who would use it (see Sarlos, 1973, pp. 65–81). Accountability tends to concentrate on behaviors and thus is informed by behavioral theory. Martin et al. argued that behavioral analysis limits education when they wrote, "because we believe that education has something to do with rational and critical thinking, introspection, and creativity, we believe that any view which confines itself exclusively to observable phenomena leaves out something essential both to the practice of science and to the process of education" (p. 6).

Besides the concern of a lack of an adequate theoretical base, basic questions dealing with accountability are not always answered. "For example, to contend that an individual or an institution ought to be accountable immediately brings to mind the questions: accountable to whom, for what, in what manner and under what circumstances?" (Wagner, 1989, p. 1). Other questions would include the following: Who should be held accountable (e.g., teachers, parents, school systems, school administrators, school teachers)? What does it mean to be accountable? When should accountability take place (e.g., grade level, proficiency level, every year)? What should be measured (e.g., knowledge, behavior, attitudes, values; see Part II)? How should accountability be measured (e.g., through portfolios, exit interviews, tests; see Part III)?

The second defect identified by Martin et al. (1976) was that accountability in education "lacks reassuring historical precedents. In fact, something very akin to accountability has been tried before and found wanting" (p. 6). They argued that the current push for accountability was only the most recent. Previous attempts had limited success.

"Third, its political implications are not reassuring to those among us who value either individuality or democracy" (Martin et al., 1976, p. 6). As stated previously, there are those who have argued that accountability, coming out of a business-training model, is not the best model for education. Bowers (1972) went so far as to argue that "teacher accountability is incompatible with academic freedom . . ." (p. 25).

> [A]ccountability proponents could argue that despite various and sometimes conflicting interpretations of accountability there is at least general agreement about the following: (1) The quality of schools can no longer be determined simply by looking at input factors such as plant facilities, the number of volumes in the library, pupil/teacher ratios or printed curricula; rather, school performance and the quality of school programs are best understood in terms of results and output, what children do or do not learn over a given period; (2) learning can be measured against costs for a specified interval as an indication of cost-effectiveness; (3) taxpayers, parents and supportive government agencies have a "right" to know about these results and the cost/benefits associated with their schools; and (4) accountability can provide this information and act as a stimulus to better school performance. (Wagner, 1989, p. 2)

Whatever the historical roots of or problems with the current accountability and assessment movements, accountability and assessment appear here to stay. (For an overview of the assessment in higher education, see Rosenbaum, 1994.)

## Forces Impacting Media Education

In the late 1980s and early 1990s, as the assessment movement continued to pick up steam (see Ervin, 1988; Ewell, Hutchings, & Marchese, 1991), at least three other challenges faced media education: calls for the reinvention of undergraduate education, the convergence of communication technologies, and the philosophical and theoretical ferment in the communication field (Blanchard & Christ, 1993; Dickson, 1995; Duncan, Caywood, & Newsom, 1993; "Planning for Curricular Change," 1984, 1987; Wartella, 1994).

It was argued that the reinvention of undergraduate education called for a "New Liberal Arts" that combined elements from both traditional and newer fields and disciplines (Blanchard & Christ, 1993). There were calls for a renewed commitment from media programs to the non-major, general student; a call for the centrality of media studies in the common curriculum of all students. As people debated what should be the outcome of an undergraduate education (see Association of American Colleges, 1985; Boyer, 1987; "Strengthening the Ties," 1988), media educators were faced with the following questions: What does my program have to offer the general university student? If one of the outcomes of a university education is to be media literate, then what should we teach and what should students learn? (see Christ & Potter, 1998).

The convergence of communication technologies and the philosophical and theoretical ferment in the communication field suggested there needed to be a new way of looking at the major. Some went so far as to demand a "New Professionalism" that educated students to become broad-based communication practitioners (Blanchard & Christ, 1993; see "Planning for Curricular Change," 1984, 1987). The calls for a broad approach to communication and media education has been both supported and attacked (see Dickson, 1995, 2000; Duncan et al., 1993; Medsger, 1996). The point is that the convergence of technologies and the philosophical and theoretical ferment in the field required media educators to reevaluate their programs to determine if what they offered made sense philosophically, pedagogically, and practically.

Overlaid on these three challenges was the assessment movement. As stated earlier, assessment, as part of the accountability movement, has been part of higher education for over 35 years. What is different now is the intensity of the current debate, where accrediting agencies seem to be taking the student learning assessment part of their charge very seriously and where legislators are willing to link funding to results. Assessment continues to be both a promise and a plague for programs as educators grapple with high expectations and limited resources (see Christ & Blanchard, 1994).

## Student Learning

A report by the Kellogg Commission on the Future of State and Land-Grant Universities (1997) demonstrates how assessment dovetails with current calls for college and university reforms. The Kellogg Commission (1997) wanted to turn schools into learning institutions. They suggested "three broad ideals":

> (1) Our institutions must become *genuine learning communities*, supporting and inspiring faculty, staff, and learners of all kinds. (2) Our learning communities should be *student centered*, committed to excellence in teaching and to meeting the legitimate needs of learners, wherever they are, whatever they need, whenever they need it. (3) Our learning communities should emphasize the importance of *a healthy learning environment* that provides students, faculty, and staff with the facilities, support, and resources they need to make this vision a reality. (pp. v–vi, italics in original)

The move from universities being conceptualized as *teaching* institutions to *learning* institutions has profound implications for higher education (cf. Christ, 1994, 1997). As universities become more focused on student learning than on teaching, more concerned with the outcomes of education than the inputs into education, then at least two things become evident. First, outcomes assessment of learning becomes a "logical" important "next step" in the process, and second, the classroom is seen as only one part, and sometimes one small part, of the total learning environment.

The shift from teaching to learning communities, from teacher-centered to student-centered approaches to education, changes the role of the classroom teacher. If, as the Kellogg Commission (1997) suggested, learning communities should be committed "to meeting the legitimate needs of learners, wherever they are, whatever they need, whenever they need it" (pp. v–vi), then it is clear that teaching and learning can no longer be confined to the classroom. And, as the costs of higher education have escalated, as more people lose access to traditional higher education opportunities (Council for Aid to Education, 1997), the idea of a 4-year residential university or college, where lectures are delivered in huge classrooms, may become an anachronism. Within all of these challenges, educators are asked to assess their programs and student learning.

## DEFINITIONS

So what is assessment? Krendl, Warren, and Reid (1997) made an interesting distinction between assessment and evaluation in their discussion about distant learning:

> Assessment refers to any process that measures what students have learned from teaching strategies, including course-specific methods (e.g., assignments, class activities, and tests) and programmatic strategies (e.g., exit interviews or honors theses) designed to test specific content knowledge. This primary focus on academic content is a defining characteristic of student assessment. Evaluation, on the other hand, looks beyond this to examine the entire educational experience. The mesh between students' needs and their experiences during a course or program is the primary criterion in evaluation. Beyond teaching strategies, then, evaluation examines classroom interaction, the effectiveness of course/program administration, the quality of student support services, access to and quality of technical equipment, and cost-benefit analyses of distance-education programs. In short, every aspect of a distance course or program can be evaluated, whereas only students' mastery of course content is assessed (Rowntree, 1992). (p. 103)

The distinction between assessment and evaluation is useful in that it directs our attention to different levels or types of accountability. Haley and Jackson (1995) suggested a hierarchy of programmatic assessment that included four levels, where

> each level may be seen as a broader examination of the program. The four levels are: Level One—Evaluation of individual program components <peer teaching review and course evaluations>; Level Two—Perceptions and performance of graduating students <survey of seniors; senior essays; university comprehensives; departmental comprehensives; campaigns courses>; Level Three—Evaluations of key internal and external constituencies <faculty surveys; employer surveys; university alumni surveys; department graduate surveys>; and Level Four—Comprehensive program evaluation <program review; accreditation>. (p. 27)

Student learning outcomes assessment is normally positioned as a level-four programmatic evaluation. Of course, to do assessment is not easy. Morse and Santiago (2000) wrote that, "to evaluate student learning adequately, faculty must set programmatic goals, understand the profiles of students, define the desired outcomes for students and programs, develop instruments to measure those outcomes, and establish a feedback loop in which the information gained is used to effective positive change" (p. 33).

# WHY ASSESSMENT?

There are two fundamental reasons for assessment. The first is external and the second is internal.

## External

As mentioned earlier, demand for assessment grew out of calls for accountability. "House (1993) proposed three different types of accountability that institutions of higher education face: state- or public-controlled accountability, professional control (by professors and administrators), and consumer control" (Krendl et al., 1997, p. 109). These three types of accountability are external to the media unit and are often seen by the unit as being harmful, coercive, or irrelevant. Under these conditions, assessment, at its best, might be seen as an antidote to calls for accountability. For example, "Lombardi (1993) posits, 'To counter-attack against criticism from the public, we need to explain and teach the public what the universities do, how they do it, and why it costs so much . . . The key weapon here is accounting' " (Haley & Jackson, 1995, p. 33). In other words, assessment is seen as a weapon to be used by the beleaguered unit to answer criticisms.

The first reason for doing assessment is that certain states, regional accrediting agencies, local administrators, professional accrediting groups, parents, and students have called for or mandated assessment. If state legislatures have developed carrots and sticks based on assessment and results, then that is an excellent reason why a unit would want to do assessment. If a unit wants to be either regionally or professionally accredited and it needs to evaluate its program and student learning outcome as part of the process, then this is an excellent reason for doing assessment. If an administration says to develop an assessment plan, then this, too, is an excellent reason for doing assessment. Ideally, a unit will be able to turn the often-odious chore of assessment into a well-articulated persuasive argument about needs and expectations. Hopefully, a unit will be able to transform all its hard work into a plan for how to improve what it does. And hopefully, a unit will be given the resources to help improve its program.

## Internal

The second reason to do assessment is that it has the potential to make teachers, programs, and ultimately, students, better. Assessment can help a unit be self-reflective about what is done and why it is done. It can mean discovering the strengths and weaknesses of programs and the teaching and learning process. "Assessment is an integral part of what we do as teachers, researchers, and administrators. It can be formal or informal, systematic or haphazard, harmful or rewarding. At its best, assessment can have a transforming effect on education. At its worst, it can be used as an instrument to punish people and programs" (Christ, 1994, p. x).

## SUMMARY

This book investigates different strategies for measuring student learning outcomes. Chapters 16 and 17 discuss a number of indirect measures for assessment including ways of using institutional data, surveys, interviews, advisory boards, internships, competitions, and career data. Chapters 18-21 identify the pros and cons of using tests, embedded "authentic" assessment, portfolios, and capstone classes. It is important that an assessment plan should link a university's mission statement with the program's mission that should confirm the program's core values, competencies, and knowledge. These core values, competencies, and knowledge should be linked to student learning outcomes which are clearly present in programs' curricula and courses and even exercises and experiences within courses. Once the student learning outcomes are articulated, then both indirect and direct methods can be developed to continually assess the outcomes. Finally, the results from the assessment should be fed back into the system.

## CONCLUSION

Ultimately, there is good assessment and bad assessment. Bad assessment is when, through lack of time, resources or will, tests or measures are thrown together to appease some outside agency or administrator. Good assessment is assessment that helps teachers and programs improve what they do so that teachers can teach and students can learn better. The American Association for Higher Education (AAHE Assessment Forum, 1997) suggests nine key "principles of good practice for assessing student learning":

1. The assessment of student learning begins with educational values; 2. Assessment is most effective when it reflects an understanding of learning as multidimensional, integrated, and revealed in performance over time; 3. Assessment works best when the programs it seeks to improve have clear, explicitly stated purposes; 4. Assessment requires attention to outcomes but also and equally to the experiences that lead to those outcomes; 5. Assessment works best when it is ongoing, not episodic; 6. As-

sessment fosters wider improvement when representatives from across the educational community are involved; 7. Assessment makes a difference when it begins with issues of use and illuminates questions that people really care about; 8. Assessment is most likely to lead to improvement when it is part of a larger set of conditions that promote change; 9. Through assessment, educators meet responsibilities to students and to the public. (pp. 11-12)

After evaluating a trial batch of student learning assessment plans from a number of Journalism and Mass Communication programs who were coming up for accreditation, the AEJMC Teaching Standards Committee (Hansen, 2004) suggested the following:

1. Assessment plans should include the unit's mission statement.
2. Assessment plans should include the "professional values and competencies" all students must master, and plans should be revised to insure they conform to the final, approved language for the "professional values and competencies" as stated in ACEJMC's . . . Accreditation Standards.
3. Assessment plans should address the means by which students will be made aware of the "professional values and competencies" as they move through the program and the major.
4. Assessment plans should reflect the concept of different levels of student learning (awareness, understanding and application). The methods used to assess student learning should indicate the level at which students are expected to perform. For example, if a direct measure is being used to evaluate student mastery of the competency of writing correctly and clearly, the measurement method should reflect the level of performance expected (most likely "application" for that competency).
5. Assessment plans should clearly identify which methods are deemed to be direct and which are deemed to be indirect measures of student learning.
6. Assessment plans should clearly link the method for measuring student learning with the appropriate "professional values and competencies" that are expected to be measured through that method.
7. Assessment plans should address the "indicators" that are articulated in Standard 9 of the new Accrediting Standards to ensure that appropriate evidence is provided for site team visitors.
8. Assessment plans should specifically articulate how the assessment effort will be staffed and maintained so that assessment is ongoing.
9. Assessment plans should specifically detail how the data collected from the direct and indirect measures will be used to improve curriculum and instruction over time.

Assessment did not just happen. It has developed within a complex of powerful forces that have continued to impact higher education. Why assessment matters is a function of both external constituencies and internal needs. The bottom line is that it is useful for media educators to address the questions: What do we want to be able to say about our students when they graduate from our program? Why do we teach what we teach? And, for assessment purposes, how do we know our students are learning what we are teaching? Hopefully, this book will help generate a discussion that will help us answer these questions.

## REFERENCES

Accrediting Council on Education in Journalism and Mass Communications. (2004). *New accrediting standards.* Retrieved July 24, 2004, from http://www.ukans.edu/~acejmc/BREAKING/New_standards_9-03.pdf

American Association for Higher Education Assessment Forum. (1997). *9 principles of good practice for assessing student learning.* Retrieved March 25, 2005, from http://www.aahe.org/assessment/principl.htm

Association of American Colleges. (1985). *Integrity in the college curriculum: A report to the academic community.* Washington, DC: Author.

Blanchard, R. O., & Christ, W. G. (1993). *Media education and the liberal arts: A blueprint for the new professionalism.* Hillsdale, NJ: Lawrence Erlbaum Associates, Inc.

Bowers, C. A. (1972). Accountability from a humanist point of view. In F. J. Sciara & R. K. Jantz (Eds.), *Accountability in American education* (pp. 25–33). Boston: Allyn & Bacon.

Boyer, E. L. (1987). *College: The undergraduate experience in America.* New York: The Carnegie Foundation for the Advancement of Teaching, Harper & Row.

Christ, W. G. (Ed.). (1994). *Assessing communication education.* Hillsdale, NJ: Lawrence Erlbaum Associates, Inc.

Christ, W. G. (Ed.). (1997). *Media education assessment handbook.* Mahwah, NJ: Lawrence Erlbaum Associates, Inc.

Christ, W. G., & Blanchard, R. O. (1994). Mission statements, outcomes and the new liberal arts. In W. G. Christ (Ed.), *Assessing communication education* (pp. 31–55). Hillsdale, NJ: Lawrence Erlbaum Associates, Inc.

Christ, W. G., McCall, J. M., Rakow, L., & Blanchard, R. O. (1997). Integrated communication programs. In W. G. Christ (Ed.), *Media education assessment handbook* (pp. 23–53). Mahwah, NJ: Lawrence Erlbaum Associates, Inc.

Christ, W. G., & Potter, W. J. (1998). Media literacy, media education, and the academy. *Journal of Communication, 48*(1), 5–15.

Council for Aid to Education. (1997). *Breaking the social contract. The fiscal crisis in higher education.* Retrieved March 25, 2005, from http://www.rand.org/publications/CAE/CAE100/index.html

Dickson, T. (1995, August). *Meeting the challenges and opportunities facing media education: A report on the findings of the AEJMC Curriculum Task Force.* Paper presented at the annual convention of the Association for Education in Journalism and Mass Communication, Washington, DC.

Dickson, T. (2000). *Mass media education in transition*. Mahwah, NJ: Lawrence Erlbaum Associates, Inc.

Duncan, T., Caywood, C., & Newsom, D. (1993, December). *Preparing advertising and public relations students for the communications industry in the 21st century*. A report of the Task Force on Integrated Curriculum.

Ervin, R. F. (1988). Outcomes assessment: The rationale and the implementation. In R. L. Hoskins (Ed.), *Insights* (pp. 19–23). Columbia, SC: Association of Schools of Journalism and Mass Communication.

Ewell, P. T., Hutchings, P., & Marchese, T. (1991). *Reprise 1991: Reprints of two papers treating assessment's history and implementation*. Washington, DC: American Association for Higher Education, Assessment Forum.

Haley, E., & Jackson, D. (1995). A conceptualization of assessment for mass communication programs. *Journalism and Mass Communication Educator, 51*, 26–34.

Hansen, K. (2004). *Accreditation guidelines for evaluating assessment of student learning plans* (Memorandum sent by the Committee on Teaching Standards chair to the chair of the Accrediting Council on Education in Journalism and Mass Communication accrediting committee).

House, E. (1993). *Professional evaluation*. Newbury Park, CA: Sage.

Janesick, V. J. (2001). *The assessment debate*. Santa Barbara, CA: AGC-CLIO, Inc.

Jones, M. G., Jones, B. D., & Hargrove, T. Y. (2003). *The unintended consequences of high-stakes testing*. Lanham, MD: Rowman & Littlefield Publishers, Inc.

Kellogg Commission on the Future of State and Land-Grant Universities. (1997). *Returning to our roots: The student experience*. Retrieved March 25, 2005, from http://www.nasulgc.org/publications/Kellogg/Kellogg2000_StudentExp.pdf

Krendl, K. A., Warren, R., & Reid, K. A. (1997). Distance learning. In W. G. Christ (Ed.), *Assessing communication education* (pp. 99–119). Mahwah, NJ: Lawrence Erlbaum Associates, Inc.

Lombardi, V. (1993). With their accounts in order, colleges can win back their critics. *The Chronicle of Higher Education, 39*, A40.

Martin, D. T., Overholt, G. E., & Urban, W. J. (1976). *Accountability in American education: A critique*. Princeton, NJ: Princeton Book Company.

McConnell, T. R. (1972). Accountability and autonomy. In F. J. Sciara & R. K. Jantz (Eds.), *Accountability in American education* (pp. 200–214). Boston: Allyn & Bacon.

Medsger, B. (1996). *Winds of change: Challenges confronting journalism education*. Arlington, VA: The Freedom Forum.

Morse, J. A., & Santiago, G., Jr. (2000). Accreditation and faculty. *Academe, 86*(1), 30–34.

National Commission on Excellence in Education. (1983). *A nation at risk: The imperative for educational reform*. Retrieved March 25, 2005, from http://www.ed.gov/pubs/NatAtRisk/index.html

No Child Left Behind Act of 2001. (2002). Public law 107-110. January 8, 2002. Retrieved March 25, 2005, from http://www.ed.gov/policy/elsec/leg/esea02/index.html

Ohmann, R. (2000). Historical reflections on accountability. *Academe, X*, 24–29.

*Planning for curricular change in journalism education*. (1984). *The Oregon Report* (Project on the Future of Journalism and Mass Communication Education). Eugene: University of Oregon, School of Journalism.

*Planning for curricular change in journalism education* (2nd ed.). (1987). The Oregon Report. (Project of the Future of Journalism and Mass Communication Education). Eugene: University of Oregon, School of Journalism.

Rosenbaum, J. (1994). Assessment: An overview. In W. G. Christ (Ed.), *Assessing communication education: A handbook for media, speech, and theatre educators* (pp. 3–29). Hillsdale, NJ: Lawrence Erlbaum Associates, Inc.

Rowntree, D. (1992). *Exploring open and distance learning*. London: Kogan Page.

Sarlos, B. (1973). The complexity of the concept 'accountability' in the context of American education. In R. L. Leight (Ed.), *Philosophers speak on accountability in education* (pp. 65–81). Danville, IL: Interstate.

*Strengthening the ties that bind: Integrating undergraduate liberal and professional study* (Report of the Professional Preparation Network). (1988). Ann Arbor: The Regents of the University of Michigan.

Wagner, R. B. (1989). *Accountability in education: A philosophical inquiry.* New York: Routledge.

Wartella, E. (1994). Foreword. In *State of the field: Academic leaders in journalism, mass communication and speech communication look to the future at the University of Texas* (p. 1). Austin: The University of Texas at Austin, College of Communication.

# Indirect Measures: Institutional Data, Surveys, Interviews, and Advisory Boards

Paul Parsons
*School of Communications*
*Elon University*

Like a mirror reflecting an image, indirect measures of assessment reflect program quality. Grades and student retention rates reflect on academic rigor. Internship supervisors assess the quality of a program through the performance of student interns. Exit interviews probe the level of satisfaction of graduating seniors, and surveys ask alumni to engage in reflective thinking about the quality of their education. An advisory board can evaluate student preparation to begin successful careers.

Together these are called indirect measures of assessment. They are "indirect" because they involve the following:

- Comparative data (grade distribution, probation and dismissal rates, student retention, graduation data).
- Outside evaluation (internships, job placement, advisory board evaluations, student performance in competitions).
- Participant reflection (student surveys, exit interviews, alumni surveys).

In contrast, "direct" measures of assessment—such as entry-level testing, departmental exams, capstone courses, and portfolio evaluation by the faculty—involve direct faculty assessment of student performance. Assessment requires the systematic digestion of meaningful data from both direct and indirect measures to improve curriculum, instruction, and student learning.

This chapter addresses the indirect measures based on institutional data, surveys, interviews, and advisory boards. The following chapter analyzes the indirect measures based on internships, competitions, and careers.

## INSTITUTIONAL DATA

Colleges and universities are awash in data. In an era of constant data collection, institutions generate so many columns of numbers that it's doubtful they all can be systematically analyzed for meaning. Banta, Lund, Black, and Oblander (1996) said the assessment challenge is not collecting data, but connecting the data so they say something meaningful. They wrote the following: "Many colleges and universities are unaware of the rich sources of information that they currently possess about their students (for example, student background characteristics, enrollment data, and course-taking patterns). Data are there to be found if one searches, yet they must be organized, manipulated, and applied in meaningful ways" (pp. 43–44).

The Accrediting Council on Education in Journalism and Mass Communications (ACEJMC) offers examples of how institutional data analysis can serve as a valuable assessment tool. For example, by regularly comparing the distribution of grades at the time of entry to the major and again at graduation, a faculty could discover fluctuations in student preparation for the major, and progress in the major, that could prompt a review of curriculum and instruction. Similarly, comparing unit and university retention rates over time "can provide helpful context for evaluating the meaning and significance of the unit's retention and graduation rates" (ACEJMC, 2001, p. 4). In addition, the Accrediting Council said that the comparison over time of data regarding student probation and dismissal can show how the unit monitors standards of student performance. This analysis could reveal skills that are consistently weak or areas within the curriculum that seem to greatly challenge students.

Let's use the E. W. Scripps School of Journalism at Ohio University as an illustration. In 2002, the Scripps School publicly documented institutional data for assessment. The data showed that 73% of journalism majors graduated within four years compared to the university average of 43%, and the average time to graduate was 4.14 years compared to 4.43 for the university (Ohio University, 2002). An earlier assessment report showed that Scripps students had a higher retention rate between the freshmen and sophomore years than the university at large, and that journalism students scored better on the university outcomes test (Ohio University, 1996).

These data reflect well on the Scripps School. But what, really, does it mean? Students in the Scripps School may have a better retention rate because they have chosen a major, compared to many at the university who are uncertain. The outcomes test shows that Scripps students are above average. Is this because of school entrance requirements? The average graduation timeline of 4.14 years is exceedingly good. If the timeline were to substantially increase, then the faculty could seek out the cause and conceivably discover that seniors were having difficulty getting the classes they needed to graduate.

The purpose of assessment is not to gather data and return "results," but to illuminate ways to strengthen curriculum, instruction, and student learning. Kinnick (1985, p. 97) asserted that institutions tend to organize reports around data, not around issues. For institutional data to have meaning in assessment, faculty and administrators must first want to know the issues they want to address.

Student retention at the university (completing a degree vs. dropping out) is one example. Institutional data have found that high school grades and standardized test scores are the best input-predictors for college retention (Astin, 1993, p. 65). A communications program could use institutional data to analyze its own retention determinants, or to focus on a particular retention subset such as minority students.

Let's say that 75% of students who enter a journalism and mass communications program graduate with a JMC major. That figure alone tells us little. If students are transferring out of the major after the first course or two, and these happen to be students with strong grade point averages (GPAs), then this is a deeply troubling retention discovery that may suggest a lack of academic quality. But if students transfer out of the unit because of poor grades or academic suspension, that would be a sign of high academic standards.

To assess its academic quality, the School of Communications at Elon University (North Carolina) monitors several institutional data points. On the front end is student selection. The School of Communications is home to 20% of Elon's student body, and institutional data show that first-year students intent on majoring in journalism and communications have a higher Scholastic Aptitude Test score than the university average (Elon University, 2005). Once enrolled, students are asked in each university class how much effort they put into the course compared to other courses. Communications students ranked courses in their major at a 4.06 on a 5-point scale compared to a 3.88 across the university.

Meanwhile, the school's GPA is below the university average (2.97 compared to 3.03). This type of data analysis can provide valuable insight into reputation and academic rigor.

A good first step in using institutional data for assessment is to conduct an inventory of the data already collected on campus, whether of students, alumni, or programs. An audit of institutional data may cause a communications unit to put two seemingly disparate data sets together to illuminate an issue. But now realism sets in. Although an audit of institutional data is laudable in theory, in practice it is likely to uncover a troubling truth: apart from data from the admissions and registrar's offices, a lot of campus data may be unusable, difficult to retrieve, or both (Astin, 1993).

## Pros and Cons

The advantages of using institutional data for assessment relate to collection and analysis. The university already gathers the data, and, if it does so regularly, trends can be detected through longitudinal analysis. The disadvantages are that the data may be difficult to retrieve or use, and, even more importantly, may not address the unit's most significant questions for assessment (see Appendix A).

## SURVEYS

Student and alumni surveys can be important indirect assessment measures. ACEJMC said the regular compilation, comparison, and analysis of student and alumni responses can help a unit assess the effectiveness of its curriculum and instruction and the quality and applicability of student learning. The goal is to discern "patterns of student and alumni judgment" about the strengths and weaknesses of a unit and the "short- and long-term usefulness or relevance" of what students learned (ACEJMC, 2001, p. 5).

A communications unit can obtain survey data in two basic ways. Universities conduct general surveys, and a unit could ask for breakout data to compare responses just from communications students or alumni. This has the advantage of no cost and no data collection and reporting; the university has already done so, and providing unit results is just a matter of typing in a variable.

The second way is for a unit to conduct its own survey of students or alumni. This offers complete control over the questions, with whatever degree of specificity a unit desires. The disadvantage is that a unit will have to write the survey, pursue an appropriate response rate, and appropriately analyze the data. A more popular option, then, may be adding questions to a university survey that only communications students or alumni would answer, providing a mechanism to merge the benefits of a large university data set for comparative purposes with the benefits of some communications specificity.

Surveys can ask low-level questions (Did you change your major while in college?) and high-level questions (Were you satisfied with the intellectual challenge of your major?). High-level questions require metacognition, the cognitive process of "thinking about thinking." Some students and alumni have the ability to deeply reflect on their learning processes and outcomes.

Student satisfaction is considered the single most important affective-psychological area for outcomes assessment (see Appendix B). This category encompasses a student's subjective college experience and perceptions of the value of that experience. Astin (1993) preferred two complementary questions, the first asking the student to express a degree of satisfaction with the overall college experience and the second posing a hypothetical question: If you could make your college choice again, would you still choose to enroll at the same institution? These two questions obviously would apply to the selection and satisfaction of the major just as easily as to the institution. Astin (1993) said that student satisfaction appears to be the only outcome measurement not heavily dependent on student input characteristics. Less-than-desired responses could lead a university or unit to host focus groups of students to try to understand the reasons for dissatisfaction.

## Graduating Seniors

A senior survey typically concentrates on three concepts: student perceptions of what they learned, teaching effectiveness, and their preparation for the professions.

Regarding the first concept, the University of Central Florida (2002) asked seniors to evaluate how their education helped them, and 86% of journalism students (given the choices of very much, somewhat, and very little) said their education helped them "very much" to be a more effective writer, whereas only 38% said "very much" about helping them become a more effective speaker.

Regarding the second and third concepts, the University of Kentucky senior survey asked students to rate (on a scale of 4 = excellent, 3 = good, 2 = fair, and 1 = poor) the quality of instruction by faculty in their major (3.34) as well as their sense of preparation for their first career job (2.77; University of Kentucky, 1999). Asking seniors who have yet to enter the job market to assess their sense of preparation could reflect positives (successful internships, student media experience) or negatives (anxiety on entering a constricted job market).

Senior surveys typically ask a variety of questions about the faculty. The University of North Carolina (1998) statewide program assessment survey asks seniors to rate (excellent, good, fair, poor) how well faculty members in their major set high expectations for learning, respect diverse ways of learning, give frequent and prompt feedback, provide career advising, and care about a student's academic success and welfare.

A survey also can help a unit scan its learning environment in other ways:

- My major offered a good range of courses.
- Courses in my major were offered when needed.
- Too many classes in my major were too large.
- Professors in my major were available for help outside of class.

The questions that a university asks reflect that university's values. At private Elon University, which places foremost emphasis on teaching, students are asked how many faculty members they personally know (62% said 5 or more, and 22% said 10 or more), and 55% of the senior class said they had been invited to a professor's home at some point in their education. These questions are seldom, if ever, found on senior surveys at large state universities. Of course, gathering data is only the first step; interpreting the date must follow, and a unit would need to benchmark its progress if it desired for graduating seniors to personally know more faculty members.

Senior surveys can provide a fountain of information to a communications faculty engaged in assessment. The University of Colorado (1998) conducted senior surveys and reported the results by major. Asked about course difficulty several years ago, 30% of journalism students said courses were too easy, 7% said they were too hard, and the rest said the level of difficulty was about right. Two years previously, 17% of journalism students had said too easy and 17% had said too hard. Considering that the sample size was substantial, these findings would be an ideal prompt for faculty members to address why their courses were increasingly being judged by seniors as too easy. Such an act of analysis, and then corrective action, is exactly what assessment is meant to accomplish.

Other questions on the Colorado instrument asked about programmatic balance. For instance, 19% of respondents said courses in the major were too theoretical, 22% said they were too practical, and the majority said they were about right. Students also said the curriculum was too flexible because few courses were required (37%) compared to those who thought the curriculum to be too rigid (4%).

Beware of the startling survey result. One university's senior survey asks lifestyle questions as well, and those results are available by major. At this particular university (politely spared identification here), the survey found that 48% of the senior class reported drinking beer frequently, compared to 62% of communications majors. Although 31% of the senior class occasionally or regularly smoked, 43% of communications majors smoked. Not surprisingly, communications majors also reported greater use, and criticism, of the campus health center. Before we laugh this one away, think about whether a communications unit should ignore or respond to such findings in an era of caring about the holistic welfare of students. Or maybe this just isn't an academic issue.

## Alumni

Alumni are prominently mentioned in the accrediting agency's assessment standard. Nowhere does it require a survey of alumni, but Standard 9 does expect that a unit "maintains contact with its alumni to assess their experiences in the professions and to gain feedback for improving curriculum and instruction" (ACEJMC, 2003, p. 11). If not by survey, then a unit must have other mechanisms for alumni feedback—perhaps a publication that invites response, or use of an alumni advisory board in the unit, or inviting back recent graduates to speak with faculty and students.

Alumni surveys have multiple benefits. Besides the positives of simply keeping in touch with former students, surveys can support assessment goals by determining how graduates perceive their education, by describing activities in which graduates are engaged, and by determining what graduates believe to be most useful in their education and what they wish they also had experienced (Shockley-Zalabak & Hulbert-Johnson, 1994, p. 304).

The University of Northern Colorado (2001) found that alumni rated their education higher than current seniors (3.5 compared to 3.1 on a 5-point scale). That may not be unusual. Alumni—especially those who have started successful careers—tend to forget the senior seminar professor who gave them grief and a C and instead remember college life fondly and credit much of their success to their college experience. In the Northern Colorado survey, 42% of journalism alumni reported employment in categories directly related to media or communications.

This raises an important question: What should the numbers be? We're all in need of benchmarks. We are swimming in numbers, but may not know if a 3.5 on a 5-point scale is good or bad, or whether 42% of graduates employed in the professions is strong or weak. We need comparison points provided either by other units on campus, or by other communications programs.

For example, first-year alumni at one state university spared identification here rated the adequacy of their educational preparation on a 7-point scale. Satisfaction by news-editorial graduates (5.29) was considerably higher than among advertising students (4.15). Comparative data like this should drive a unit to investigate why advertising students were considerably less positive. In open-ended comments, advertising students said they needed more skills in the classroom and more help with career planning. These were survey findings crying out for an assessment corrective.

Many universities administer an alumni survey 6 months or so after graduation, typically to assess if graduates have obtained meaningful employment and if the university's career center was effective in helping them. As a general benchmark, many communications units will be pleased if half or more of its graduates report media-related occupations, with the other half in private business, law or graduate school, nonprofit sectors, still seeking, or not seeking.

Surveys, of course, can be expensive and produce a low response rate. Orlik and Donald (1997) wrote how the broadcast department at Central Michigan University decided not to conduct alumni questionnaires for budgetary reasons: "Tracking all of these graduates, delivering a valid questionnaire to them, and then tabulating and analyzing the results were tasks far beyond the resources of an already multi-activity department served by a single secretary" (pp. 56–57). The faculty feared that results would be skewed anyway—too positive if only successful graduates took the initiative to stay in touch, or too negative if mailings went to parents' homes where alumni were once again living because they hadn't secured decent-paying positions.

Response rates are a significant issue, and that hinges on survey method and timing. The University of Massachusetts (2002) administered a one-page senior survey as students picked up caps and gowns, with a 63% completion rate. Northern Colorado (2001) reported a 74% response by graduating seniors hand-delivered a survey, and a 32% response by alumni to a mailed survey. The University of Colorado (1999) journalism school had a 30% alumni response 8 months after graduation. Online surveys hold additional promise, but all survey methods face similar problems with response-rate validity.

Northern Arizona University (2003) conducts a telephone survey of about 400 seniors each year to assess their level of educational satisfaction. As is common in survey research, women and Whites were overrepresented as survey respondents. Men and minorities simply tend to respond at a lower rate. To give a sense of the discrepancy, Northern Arizona reported that 65% of survey respondents were women (compared to 59% of all graduating seniors) and 80% were White (compared to 75% of all seniors).

Although a survey is an ideal tool to measure how seniors or alumni perceive their education, it is difficult for a survey to measure program impact. This can be accomplished only by comparing an outcome measure with a pretest or a predicted outcome based on the characteristics of entering students.

**Pros and Cons.** Surveys provide quantitative results for comparison and can be administered to all students or alumni, or to a subset if desired. Another advantage is the growing acceptance of online surveys, whose only cost is in the initial setup. Traditional surveys have always had the disadvantage of cost—either the cost of printing and mailing, or the cost and time-intensiveness of phone surveys. Other disadvantages are the possibility of low response rates, historically true among men and minorities, and no possibility of following up on responses.

## EXIT INTERVIEWS

An exit interview of graduating seniors is an "indirect" measure when it is akin to a survey, with self-assessment questions that ask students their level of satisfaction with the major and whether they feel prepared to start a career.

However, an exit interview would be a "direct" measure if the faculty used it to assess levels of awareness and application of subject content, a la the following: (a) What research steps would make a public opinion poll trustworthy? (b) describe "fair use" in copyright law, and (c) demonstrate the differences in writing for print and broadcast.

Just as portfolio assessment by faculty is a direct measure, this form of an exit interview would essentially be a "portfolio-in-the-head" assessment. Limburg (1994) said this form of exit interview also could include reviewing and critiquing student assignments in key courses, assessing the degree of improvement in a student's work from program entry to exit, and identifying strengths and weaknesses in the student's overall performance. At Ball State (2005), all seniors undergo an exit interview in which they prepare a professional employment portfolio for critical evaluation by a sequence coordinator.

This chapter assumes that an exit interview is an indirect measure similar to a survey. ACEJMC (2001, p. 5) said exit interviews, over time, can show patterns of student judgment concerning the strengths and weaknesses in curriculum, instruction, and student learning.

An exit interview is typically a sit-down conversation with the dean, department chair, faculty member, adviser, or designated local professional (see Appendix C). The interview focuses on the acquisition of cognitive, behavioral, and affective skills and knowledge, and how this acquisition relates to expected career requirements. Here are examples of appropriate questions for an exit interview:

- What was the best course you took in the major, and why?
- Do you believe you wrote enough papers, read enough books, and spoke enough in your classes?
- Have your future plans and your view of life changed since you began studying here?
- What advice would you give to an incoming freshman in your major?

Cumulative responses can be illuminating. One program learned that so many teachers and visiting professionals talked so much about the negatives of a broadcast journalism career (odd hours, low pay, deadline pressure) that some students chose another academic area. The faculty realized they needed to highlight the positives (importance to society, exciting career, access to decision makers) in an equal proportion. This is a way of using exit-interview results to improve instruction.

An exit interview is so much more personal than a survey. Students may open up a lot more in person, providing insights that never would have been made on paper or online. An interview also allows for two-way conversation, allowing a questioner to follow up on a point or to probe for an issue still under the surface. Of course, an interview is time consuming and requires extensive note taking for data collection. Some students also may be shy or intimidated, and might be more forthright in sharing information on paper than under a personal gaze.

In conducting an interview, start with an icebreaker question that requires a student to tell a story. A good one is as follows: "How did you choose your major?" Look for open-ended questions that encourage plenty of expression. It is more important to listen than to write. Take note of the ideas, but it's not essential to get exact quotes. In an interview setting of three or more, establish a policy that when weaknesses in the program are cited, no specific faculty names should be used, but note the semester and year in which the course was taken. Save the hardest questions for the latter part of the interview. A recommended final question is as follows: "If you had a magic wand, what would you change in your major?"

When initiating exit interviews in 1996, the College of Journalism at the University of South Carolina conducted two focus group sessions with about 15 graduating seniors each. Questions focused on the degree to which students felt prepared to enter the professional workforce, which academic experiences prepared them well (or not at all) for their careers, and their ability to articulate ethical and social values in communications (VanSlyke Turk, 1997).

Sometimes the exit interview is tied to a course. At the University of Missouri (2005), an assessment of advertising seniors occurs through the capstone course Strategic Communication Campaigns, where each student has a 30-min interview with a working professional. Although students may use the opportunity to practice interviewing skills or plug for a job, the university said that the interview is designed to assess the Advertising Department's program. The university instructs the professionals to differentiate between a student's likes–dislikes and the program's strengths–shortcomings. The University of Missouri Web site said the following of senior assessment: "Some students may not realize the value of some courses and activities until they have been out of the program for a year or more. Or, some students may have had different expectations than what the program actually was intended to deliver. Even in these instances, though, knowing this type of information might indicate we need to be more upfront about what our program covers" (University of Missouri, 2005). The professionals write a report based on collective student interviews. When all senior assessments have been conducted, the department chair shares the group findings with the advertising faculty, and the department identifies how to use the feedback to improve the program.

Some universities require seniors to complete a pre-interview written evaluation followed by the actual interview. Other programs tie the interview to a specific purpose. In 2002, the journalism program at the University of Wisconsin (2002) conducted exit interviews with the first students to complete its new curriculum.

Although exit interviews typically focus on the major, a few universities formalize the exit-interview process across campus. The University of Kansas (2002) selects students through a stratified random sample balanced by academic major and demographics. Students are paid to undergo a 45-min interview, and they do not know the questions in advance. Three faculty members rate each student following questions such as the following: What have you learned in your classes about the history of race relations in this country? What was the most important technology of the 20th century, and why? What do you think it means to be a good citizen, and would you describe yourself as one? The questions are designed to discern curricular weaknesses across campus and provide a university-wide comparison of schools and colleges. For example, journalism students at the university cumulatively scored above the university cohort in understanding diversity.

**Pros and Cons.** Interviews are a highly personal form of assessment. Open-ended questions encourage detailed answers, and two-way conversation allows for follow-up questions. On the negative side, individual interviews are time consuming and small-group interviews require a skilled facilitator. Some students may not fully participate, and collectively making sense of what students say requires extensive note taking and analysis.

## ADVISORY BOARDS

A communications unit can obtain assessment feedback from advisory boards of all types. The most common is an alumni board, or a combination of alumni and working professionals. Some units involve community members as well, and there's a growing trend toward establishing student advisory boards.

The Journalism Alumni Board at Indiana University (2004) usually meets twice a year, with the fall meeting tied to Homecoming. The dean provides a school update, and alumni and professionals talk about ways to improve the school, such as having a mentoring program for recent graduates as they enter the workplace.

Ohio University invites journalism professionals to conduct mock job interviews during Communications Week. The advisory board's function is to advise the faculty on curriculum, professional needs, and industry trends. The school credited the board's conversations with students as leading to a dramatic expansion of computer lab availability, the addition of public speaking to the curriculum, the assignment of a graduate student to do daily critiques of the campus newspaper, and regular programs for students on how to find a job and succeed in the professional world (Ohio University, 1996).

Although professionals usually are gentle with individual students, they can be tough evaluators as a whole. Guiniven (1998) asked senior public relations executives to evaluate the skills of new graduates entering the field. Half gave graduates as a whole an A or B for media knowledge (understanding deadlines, the reporter's job, media's role in society), and the other half gave new graduates a C or below. Only 14% of the executives gave new graduates an A or B for business knowledge (basic economics, finance, marketing), whereas 38% gave new graduates a D or F. The writing skills of new graduates also did not overly impress public relations executives, with 43% giving new graduates an A or B, 40% a C, and 17% a D or F.

There's a lot to be said for presence. If professionals are speaking in classes, talking with students, having coffee with professors, walking the campus, looking at bulletin boards, and seeing the energy in the hallways, professionals are more likely to be enthusiastic about the education of communications students. When professionals have no connection with a college or university, it's understandable that they might form opinions based on a weaker new employee and become long-distance critics of what they do not see.

A professional advisory board adds excitement when it comes to campus. Knowing that newspaper editors, broadcast news directors, and corporate vice presidents have taken a day to come to campus heightens for students the importance of their ongoing education, especially if these professionals will be guests in their classes or conduct mock interviews of seniors.

Formally connecting a group of professionals to the communications unit can build relationships between the university and external constituencies. Christ, Orlik, and Tucker (1999) observed that an active advisory board is an indication of a unit that is "dynamic and outward-looking instead of sedentary and parochial" (p. 384). But the board will not succeed unless it has clearly focused goals. When professionals come to campus, they want to believe they make a difference. If they only hear reports and have lunches and then go home, they may not return.

An advisory board, then, needs to have an agenda. A dean or department head must think through how to use the board for programmatic good. That's why assessment roles seem ideally suited to an advisory board. Professionals or alumni can interview seniors, or do portfolio assessments, or speak in classes. If the unit can gather systematic feedback from the visitors, then the unit has created a useful assessment vehicle. Besides the ever-widening web of networking, Christ et al. (1999) said the presence of an advisory board "formalizes this feedback" (p. 384) for the purposes of assessment.

Advisory boards come in all shapes, sizes, and purposes. At the time of this writing, Bowling Green State (2005) had a 20-member Alumni

Advisory Board that examined final student projects from the department's capstone courses. The University of Georgia's Grady College (2005) had a 23-member advisory board with individual members and corporate members (such as CNN News Group, *Atlanta Journal-Constitution*, Cox Enterprises, and J. Walter Thompson). The University of Nevada at Reno (2005) journalism advisory board included 21 working professionals, 11 of them alumni. At the University of Iowa (2005), 25 of the 34 advisory board members for the School of Journalism and Mass Communications were alumni.

Although an advisory board consisting of alumni and working professionals is the most common, don't overlook the opportunity for assessment by a student advisory board that meets monthly with the dean or department head to provide systematic evaluation of the program. A student board should tilt toward juniors and seniors (and graduate students if a graduate degree is offered). A student group can be a sounding board for new ideas and for implementation procedures. Although few communications programs have community members as part of an advisory board, this could change as programs increasingly seek local service-learning opportunities for their students.

## Pros and Cons

Using advisory boards for assessment connects students with working professionals, measures students against professional expectations, and builds relationships between the unit and external constituencies. Among the disadvantages, outsiders will have less knowledge of curriculum and instruction and therefore will not make the same connections that faculty would, and weak students may reflect negatively on the unit. Also, the unit must gather systematic feedback from advisory board members for meaningful analysis.

## CONCLUSION

Each communications program is distinctive. Each should handpick the indirect assessment measures listed in this chapter (and the following) that best fit the mission, goals, objectives, and values of that program. Banta et al. (1996) noted that "assessment cannot and should not take place in the absence of a clear sense as to what matters most at the institution. Indeed, in order for assessment to lead to improvements, it must reflect what people are passionate about, committed to, and value" (p. 5). As Astin (1993) observed, assessment efforts should not be concerned about valuing that which can be measured, but instead measuring that which is valued.

# REFERENCES

Accrediting Council on Education in Journalism and Mass Communications. (2001). *A guide to assessment of student learning.* Lawrence, KS: Author.

Accrediting Council on Education in Journalism and Mass Communications. (2003). *Standards of accreditation* (adopted September 2003). Lawrence, KS: Author.

Astin, A. W. (1993). *Assessment for excellence: The philosophy and practice of assessment and evaluation in higher education.* New York: American Council on Education/Oryx Press.

Ball State University. (2005). Personal interview with journalism department chair Marilyn Weaver, July 21, 2005.

Banta, T. W., Lund, J. P., Black, K. E., & Oblander, F. W. (1996). *Assessment in practice: Putting principles to work on college campuses.* San Francisco: Jossey-Bass.

Bowling Green State University. (2002). *Assessment report, 2001–02.* Retrieved July 21, 2005, from http://www.bgsu.edu/offices/provost/Assessment/Journalism2002.htm

Christ, W. G., Orlik, P. B., & Tucker, D. (1999). Self-studies, external reviews, and programmatic assessment. In W. G. Christ (Ed.), *Leadership in times of change: A handbook for communication and media administrators* (pp. 377–397). Mahwah, NJ: Lawrence Erlbaum Associates, Inc.

Elon University. (2005). Compiled by chapter author at his home institution.

Guiniven, J. E. (1998). Public relations executives view the curriculum: A needs assessment. *Journalism & Mass Communication Educator, 52,* 48–55.

Indiana University. (2004). *Dear alumni.* Retrieved March 8, 2005, from http://www.journalism.indiana.edu/alumni/newswire/archives/volXXVIIno1/stories/letter.html

Kinnick, M. K. (1985). Increasing the use of student outcomes information In P. T. Ewell (Ed.), *Assessing educational outcomes* (pp. 93–109). San Francisco: Jossey-Bass.

Limburg, V. E. (1994). Internships, exit interviews, and advisory boards. In W. G. Christ (Ed.), *Assessing communication education: A handbook for media, speech, and theatre educators* (pp. 181–200). Hillsdale, NJ: Lawrence Erlbaum Associates, Inc.

Northern Arizona University. (2003). *Trends in graduating senior satisfaction.* Flagstaff, AZ: Author.

Ohio University. (1996). *E. W. Scripps School assessment report.* Retrieved March 8, 2005, from http://www.ohiou.edu/instres/assessments/95_96assess/dept/jour.html

Ohio University. (2002). *Six-year graduation rates.* Retrieved March 8, 2005, from http://www.ohiou.edu/instres/student/gradratecoll97.html

Orlik, P. B., & Donald, R. (1997). Telecommunications programs. In W. G. Christ (Ed.), *Media education assessment handbook* (pp. 55–78). Mahwah, NJ: Lawrence Erlbaum Associates, Inc.

Shockley-Zalabak, P., & Hulbert-Johnson, R. (1994). Organizational communication. In W. G. Christ (Ed.), *Assessing communication education: A handbook for media, speech & theatre educators* (pp. 291–310). Hillsdale, NJ: Lawrence Erlbaum Associates, Inc.

University of Central Florida. (2002). *Graduating senior survey.* Retrieved March 8, 2005, from http://www.2oeas.ucf.edu/oeas2/SurveyProgram/journalism.htm

University of Colorado. (1998). *Senior survey.* Retrieved March 8, 2005, from http://www.colorado.edu/pba/surveys/senior/98/by_coll/jourtab.htm

University of Colorado. (1999). *School of Journalism and Mass Communication.* Retrieved March 8, 2005, from http://www.colorado.edu/pba/outcomes/units/jour.htm

University of Georgia. (2005). *Grady College advisory board.* Retrieved July 21, 2005, from http://www.grady.uga.edu/about_grady.php?al1=About+Grady&al2=Advisory+Board&page=advisory_board.inc.php

University of Iowa. (2005). *Professional advisory board*. Retrieved July 21, 2005, from http://www.uiowa.edu/jmc/people/advisory.html

University of Kansas. (2002). *Report on the 2002 assessment of General Education*. Lawrence, KS: Office of Institutional Research and Planning.

University of Kentucky. (1999). *Graduating senior survey*. Lexington, KY: Office of Assessment and Institutional Data.

University of Massachusetts. (2002). *Graduating senior survey 2000–2002*. Amherst, MA: Office of Academic Planning and Assessment.

University of Missouri. (2005). *Senior assessment guidelines*. Retrieved March 5, 2005, from http://www.journalism.missouri.edu/undergrad/senior-assessment.html

University of Nevada at Reno. (2005). *RSJ advisory board*. Retrieved July 21, 2005, from http://www.unr.edu/journalism/peo.advisory.html

University of North Carolina. (1998). *UNC program assessment*. Retrieved March 8, 2005, from http://www.ga.unc.edu/UNCGA/assessment/uncsurveys/gss_across.html

University of Northern Colorado. (2001). *Annual assessment profiles*. Retrieved March 8, 2005, from http://asweb.unco.edu/Profiles/2000-2001/jmc.htm

University of Wisconsin. (2002). *New curriculum well under way and looking successful thus far* (letter from director Sharon Dunwoody). Retrieved January 1, 2004, from http://www.journalism.wisc.edu/alumni/documents/wj_spring02/director_spring02.html

VanSlyke Turk, J. (1997). Journalism and mass communication programs. In W. G. Christ (Ed.), *Media education assessment handbook* (pp. 79–98). Mahwah, NJ: Lawrence Erlbaum Associates, Inc.

# APPENDIX A

## Pros and Cons of Using Each Measure

### Institutional Data

Pro:   Data already collected
Allow for longitudinal analysis

Con:   May be difficult to retrieve or use
May not apply to the unit's important questions

### Surveys

Pro:   Provide quantitative results for comparison
Can be administered to all students or alumni
Online surveys growing more common, at little cost

Con:   Printing and mailing of surveys expensive
Low response rates, especially among men and minorities
No possibility of following up on responses

### Interviews

Pro:   Highly personal
Open-ended questions encourage fuller answers
Two-way conversation allows for follow-up questions

Con:   Time-consuming
       Requires extensive note-taking for data collection
       Some students may be shy or intimidated

## Advisory Boards

Pro:   Measure students against professional expectations
       Connect students with working professionals
       Build relationships between unit and external constituencies
Con:   Less knowledge of curriculum and instruction
       Weak students may reflect negatively on the unit
       Must gather systematic feedback for meaningful analysis

# APPENDIX B

## Questions That Can Be Answered With Each Measure

## Institutional Data

- How does the rigor of the unit compare to the university, as defined by grade point average, student dismissal rates, or a university outcomes test?
- How has retention changed over time?
- How does the unit's job placement compare to the university at large?

## Surveys

- What is the level of student satisfaction with the major?
- Did the unit offer a good range of courses, available when needed?
- How well did the faculty set high expectations for learning, give prompt feedback, and care about a student's academic success and welfare?
- What do alumni believe was most useful in their education?

## Interviews

- What would students preserve or change in the major, and why?
- What is their sense of preparation for the first job?

- Did their career plans, or view of life, evolve since becoming a major?
- What advice would students give to incoming freshmen in the major?

## Advisory Boards

- Do students impress professionals with their knowledge and skills?
- Do seniors have appropriate portfolios to enter the job market?

# APPENDIX C

## Steps in Using Each Measure

### Institutional Data

1. Conduct an inventory of data already available on campus.
2. Determine if the data address important issues to the unit.
3. If so, identify who can help with data retrieval and analysis.
4. Suggest inclusion of specific assessment questions for future institutional research.

### Surveys

1. Decide what you want to learn from students or alumni.
2. Study surveys conducted by others to help with question wording.
3. Select the survey method (mail, phone, online) that best accomplishes your goal within your limitations (budget, time, staffing).
4. Conduct a census or randomized sampling based on population size.
5. Analyze data against predetermined benchmarks.

### Interviews

1. Draft faculty, administrators, or others to interview selected students.
2. Select students to reflect the demographics of the unit.
3. Decide whether to interview individually or in small groups.
4. If using small groups, select a skilled facilitator to lead discussions.
5. If individually, create some common questions for consistency.

6. Ask open-ended questions and follow up for detailed answers.
7. Report key findings in aggregate form.

## Advisory Boards

1. Invite professionals or alumni to conduct mock job interviews.
2. Create common questions that allow for individual detours.
3. Gather their feedback, preferably before they leave campus.
4. Report key findings to the faculty for a programmatic discussion.

# Indirect Measures: Internships, Careers, and Competitions

Don A. Grady
*School of Communications*
*Elon University*

The success of an academic program can be reflected in the success of students in external environments. This chapter examines the use of outside evaluations—internships, job placement, and student performance in competitions—as forms of indirect measurement. The previous chapter discussed other indirect measures: analysis of comparative data based on regular university compilations, self-assessment (student surveys, exit interviews, and alumni surveys), and advisory boards.

Indirect measures are based, in large part, on the assessment of student outcomes. It is the evaluation of what students know and how well they are able to perform. Whether outcomes are measured incrementally within courses, as separate courses within a curriculum, or at completion of a program, the key issue is the ability of the academic program to influence student learning. Thus, assessment requires that an academic program examine how well it achieves its goals and objectives. In addition, the assessment process may reveal unexpected information that may be useful in establishing new goals and objectives. Clearly, the ability of a program to demonstrate that it is successful in this regard is found in part in student learning, and hence, outcomes.

## PROFESSIONAL ORIENTATION AND ASSESSMENT

Many journalism and mass communications programs recognize the centrality of the liberal arts to their mission. This centrality is emphasized by the Accrediting Council on Education in Journalism and Mass

Communications' (ACEJMC) "80/65" rule, which requires a minimum of 80 credit hours outside the unit with at least 65 of those credit hours in the liberal arts and sciences outside of the unit. However, most academic units also admit to having a clear professional orientation. Many academic programs either mention this professional orientation in their mission statement, or in one of the goals or objectives in their assessment plan. For example, the first item listed in the Texas Tech School of Communication mission statement is to "educate students in the knowledge, skills and perspectives necessary for future careers in communications industries" (Texas Tech University, p. 1). The first sentence in the assessment plan for the University of Georgia (2003) is as follows: "The Department of Journalism in the College of Journalism and Mass Communications helps student prepare for careers in magazines, newspapers, specialized publications, news services, journalism education, and other employment areas" (p. 1). The first goal in the Learning Outcomes Assessment statement of the Cronkite School at Arizona State University (2002–2003) is as follows: "The primary mission . . . is to prepare students to enter positions in media fields" (p. 1).

It must be acknowledged that not all schools claim a professional orientation. Nevertheless, the notion that a practical orientation is favored in the classroom and the workplace is supported by the findings of a study of broadcast journalism curricula. Duhe and Zukowski (1997) found that both academics and industry professionals prefer a "five-day-a-week" news laboratory experience over a liberal arts-journalism model or a classic liberal arts model.

A professional orientation also is reflected in ACEJMC Standard 2, which includes a list of "Professional Values and Competencies" for all graduates, regardless of specialization. Among these "core values and competencies" are the following specific references to the profession:

- Demonstrate an understanding of the history and role of *professionals* and institutions in shaping communications.
- Demonstrate an understanding of *professional* ethical principles and work ethically in pursuit of truth, accuracy, fairness and diversity.
- Conduct research and evaluate information by methods appropriate to the communications *professions* in which they work.
- Apply tools and technologies appropriate for communications *professions* in which they work. (ACEJMC, 2003 p. 3, emphasis added)

Clearly, a professional orientation in journalism and mass communications programs is alive and well, and many programs proudly state that one of their primary goals is to prepare graduates for entry-level positions in the field.

Many different types of assessment occur in an academic community. It may be helpful to consider indirect measures of assessment in terms of "perspective." Astin (1993) identified six perspectives for assessing outcomes: departmental, disciplinary, "state," student, professional, and employer. He noted how the relation between curriculum and outcome assessment is affected by the first two perspectives: "under the departmental perspective we tend to 'test what we teach,' whereas under the disciplinary perspective we are more inclined to 'teach to the test' " (p. 39). The "state" perspective on outcome relates to "minimal competencies" such as reading, writing, and computation skills. The "student" perspective examines the responsiveness of a program in meeting the "personal goals and aspirations" of students. Of the six perspectives, the two that seem most pertinent to this discussion of indirect measures for assessing academic programs are the "professional" and "employer" perspectives. The professional perspective, Astin wrote, "attempts to assess those outcomes that are relevant to entry to a profession or professional school" (p. 39), whereas the employer perspective is concerned with the "skills and personal qualities most valued by the employer of our graduates" (p. 40). Thus, these two perspectives are concerned with "value." The indirect measures discussed later examine how professionals and employers value and evaluate the knowledge and skills of students from their perspective outside the institution.

This chapter looks at three types of indirect measures based on a professional orientation: internships, careers, and competitions. They are all based on evaluations outside the academic unit. Indirect measures of these external experiences may be useful as "indicators" of student learning. In fact, ACEJMC Standard 9 recommends that such indirect measures be included in an academic unit's written assessment plan (ACEJMC, 2003). Although the collection and analysis of data related to these activities may seem anecdotal, ACEJMC recognizes that such information may prove useful in gauging the overall effectiveness of curriculum and instruction in preparing students to work in journalism and mass communications professions. According to the Accrediting Council, "this information does not measure the nature and amount of student learning, so much as indicate that learning has occurred" (ACEMJC, 2001, p. 3). In this way, professional-employer derived external measures reflect the strengths and weaknesses of an academic program.

## INTERNSHIPS

The internship is one form of experiential education that is designed to extend the classroom beyond the walls of the university. As an indirect measure in assessment, the internship may provide valuable information about student learning. As listed in ACEJMC Standard 2, internships and professional experiences outside the classroom are "indicators" which may be used in assessment, as evidenced by records and statistics (ACEJMC, 2003, p. 3). As discussed earlier, the rationale behind this guideline seems apparent: that many journalism and communications programs, although firmly rooted in the liberal arts, have a clear professional orientation. Thus, an academic unit, accredited or not, will find the internship helpful in assessing the overall impact of the program.

An internship is an opportunity to connect theory and practice. It is an opportunity to associate what is learned in the classroom with the realities of the profession. Katula and Threnhauser (1999) suggested two general purposes for internships: "to offer students an understanding of organizational structures and protocol within a professional working environment" and, "to provide students an opportunity for professional development" (p. 247). More specifically, internships are helpful in making contacts, establishing references, building a resume, enhancing knowledge, improving writing and production skills, and providing access to professional-level equipment. Perhaps most pertinent to this discussion, internships are an opportunity for program assessment. Internships should have intentional learning objectives, require careful supervision by an academic coordinator and work-site supervisor, and have a structured evaluation process. As such, internships present themselves as readily available and valid indicators of the success or failure of an academic unit in achieving its goals and objectives.

The affiliation requirements for some professional organizations even mandate completion of an internship. For example, one of the six requirements for establishing a chapter of the Public Relations Student Society of America (PRSSA; n.d., p. 1) is a "supervised public relations experience (internship)." Many journalism and communication programs and employers believe that an internship is essential for students who are serious about working in the profession. According to a PRSSA commissioned study, 90% of public relations professionals surveyed believe that internships are "quite or very important" (Gibson, 1998, p. 2).

The perceived value of an internship is supported by research that shows a large number of institutions allow or require an internship. Many programs assist students in locating appropriate internship opportunities and grant academic credit (Basow & Byrne, 1993). As a result, a high percentage of students complete an internship before graduation. An Internet survey of Broadcast Education Association (BEA) institutions indicated that nearly all students completed an internship in the one third of schools where it is required, and about 40% completed an internship in the remaining two thirds of schools that do not require an internship (Shriver, 2004). Overall, this means about 60% of the students completed an internship at schools responding to the BEA survey.

## Implementation of Internships

Although internships are encouraged by professionals and valued by students and academics, implementation practices vary widely by academic program. A number of important issues must be resolved if internships are to be used in assessment, including the following: whether to allow or require an internship, the number of academic credit hours required or permitted, the value and commitment to experiential learning in the curriculum, and factors that contribute to successful administration of internships, including academic preparedness and worksite supervision.

The decisions to allow or require internships, to grant academic credit, and the amount of credit, may be complex in the context of overall curricular requirements and ACEJMC constraints, where applicable. In encouraging supervised professional experiences outside the classroom, the ACEJMC Standard on Curriculum and Instruction is as follows:

> Schools may award academic credit for internships in fields related to journalism and mass communications, but credit should not exceed one semester course (or its equivalent) if the internship is away from the institution, and, for the most part, supervised by media professionals rather than academics.
>
> Students may take up to two semester courses (or their equivalent) at an appropriate professional organization where the unit can show ongoing and extensive dual supervision by the unit's faculty and professionals.
>
> Students may take up to three semester courses (or their equivalent) at a professional media outlet owned and operated by the institution where full-time faculty are in charge and where the primary function of the media outlet is to instruct students. (ACEJMC, 2003, p. 4)

Many academic programs either allow or require internships for academic credit. But the issue of academic credit is complicated by the fact that many, if not most, employers require that interns receive either credit or compensation (Whitlow, 2003). This restriction is based on Fair Labor Standards Act guidelines for nonpaying positions, such as trainees and volunteers. Students who are paid become employees. Because many employers refuse to pay interns and some view interns as free labor, students may find themselves paying tuition to work without pay. This awkward combination of circumstances makes it difficult for many programs to justify required internships. Although some students may want academic credit, others may not, because academic credit (particularly in summer school) usually involves additional tuition fees.

In examining the "credit versus no-credit issue" as implemented in selected internships programs, Whitlow (2003) found that some programs, such as the University of Illinois Journalism Department and the S.I. Newhouse School of Public Communication at Syracuse University, give academic credit because it is required by many employers. Although some programs require that credit be granted during the academic term of the internship experience, others, such as the one at the University of Illinois, link summer school experience to credit in a fall course so students can avoid additional tuition fees. Most programs generally allow one internship for 1 to 3 hours of credit, according to Whitlow. Also, most schools require a minimum number of work hours for each credit hour granted.

Some academic units require an internship because it communicates that these programs value experiential education. However, the decision to require internships commits programs to ensuring that well structured internship experiences are available for all majors. For example, the School of Communications at Elon University established a requirement that all majors complete either an internship for academic credit or a noncredit "professional work experience." Although there are academic requirements for both types of experiences, students receive credit for an internship and a "check-off" for a noncredit work experience. To ensure the successful implementation of the program and assist students in finding quality internship and work experience situations off campus, the School of Communications employs a full-time director of internships. One rationale for this level of commitment is that internships are an opportunity for a supervised indirect external measure for program assessment.

When administered successfully, an internship has been shown to be an effective tool in the curriculum for learning and assessment. A number of factors may contribute to a successful internship. One study of advertising and public relations students in accredited journalism and mass communications programs examined the relation between the success of the internship field experience and six predictors of internship success: academic preparedness, proactive-aggressiveness, positive attitude, quality of worksite supervision, organizational practices and policies, and compensation (Beard & Morton, 1999). Generally, these predictors were correlated with internship success, and the study found that "a large proportion of students had what they believe to be a successful internship" (Beard & Morton, 1999, p. 50). Of the six predictors, "the quality of supervision and organizational practices and policies ... proved to be the best predictor of a successful internship" (Beard & Morton, 1999, pp. 50–51). Notably, the study found that proactivity-aggressiveness and compensation were "moderately correlated" with internship success, that academic preparedness "proved considerably less important than other predictors," and that an internship did not lead to an increase in career focus (Beard & Morton, p. 51). Although these findings may challenge some assumptions made by some programs, the study affirms the importance of a well structured and supervised internship program.

Clearly, requirements and practices at the worksite contribute to the success of an internship. These include the opportunity to do meaningful work, the level of supervision, and the seriousness and quality of the supervisor evaluation. On the other hand, employer grievances tend to focus on interns' "lack of preparation, training and motivation" (Katula & Threnhauser, 1999, p. 248).

Despite the mixed messages about the importance of preparedness discussed earlier, academic programs and employers typically want students to be prepared before embarking on an internship. In his study of selected programs, Whitlow (2003) found that all programs had some type of prerequisite: "Internship prerequisites most commonly involve grade point average (GPA), the completion of specific courses, and/or the completion of a minimum number of academic credits (junior standing is a common expectation)" (p. 343). Although GPA and minimum credit hours may be useful in controlling the flow of marginal interns into the workplace, course preparation is thought to be critical and should be linked to the goals and objectives of an academic unit's curriculum.

Obviously, some internship sites have more highly structured programs than others, and the quality of supervision varies greatly. It seems clear that academic programs have an obligation to work closely with employers in establishing and maintaining guidelines to achieve learning objectives. These guidelines should focus and constrain student interns and worksite supervisors. Katula and Threnhauser (1999) noted the following:

> An internship which serves as a form of experiential education must be more than simply "work for credit." An internship program must be integrated into the curriculum by trained faculty, and it must adhere to the learning principles upon which its inherent legitimacy is based. When properly developed and instituted, an internship program can become a useful learning tool in the undergraduate curriculum. (p. 248)

## Assessment of Internships

As an indirect measure for assessment, the cumulative performance of students who have completed an internship must be considered by the academic unit. At one level, assessment is concerned with evaluating the work of individual students. The end result of this evaluation is a grade in the course. At another level, data acquired from the evaluation of individual student interns may be used to establish records and to generate statistics for the purpose of making comparisons in program assessment.

As required by ACEJMC standards, internships and professional experiences must be supervised and evaluated when students are awarded academic credit. Academic work requirements for an internship might include the following:

- Daily or weekly diary, journal, or calendar of events.
- Description or discussion of formal and informal tasks completed.
- Reports on books or readings pertinent to employer or type of work.
- Portfolio of work completed during internship.
- Papers based on interviews with significant personnel in the company or organization.
- Final report or reflection paper.
- Debriefing session with academic supervisor.
- Worksite supervisor evaluation.
- Student evaluation of the worksite and internship experience.

Items on the aforementioned list are useful for outcomes assessment of the learning goals and objectives of a student internship. Completion of these and other requirements enables the academic supervisor to make a reasonable evaluation of an intern's work in the field and determine a fair grade in a for-credit internship.

To be useful in program assessment, the information acquired through this evaluation process must be linked to the goals and objectives established in the academic program assessment plan, showing that student learning has occurred. A typical intern evaluation form completed by a worksite supervisor might include questions related to dependability, creativity, initiative, appearance, self-confidence, emotional stability, communication skills, professional skills, pride in work, speed, and accuracy (Gross, 1981). Responses to these items may indicate something about the character of a student, but they also should link to the goals and objectives of an academic program. Where does the program teach the values of dependability, initiative, pride in work, and self-confidence? Does the program inform students about appearance? If these are not clearly defined objectives in the curriculum, why should an intern be evaluated on these items? Although "communication skills" and "professional skills" seem most directly pertinent to the evaluation of a journalism or communication intern, the framing of these items may be so general that they say little about what an intern has been able to contribute in a professional setting.

Broadly framed questions may reveal little about how these skills reflect the goals and objectives of a curriculum. More specific questions, such as queries about writing ability and productions skills, must be included if an evaluation instrument is to be helpful in program assessment. For example, the Cronkite School of Journalism and Mass Communication at Arizona State University asked worksite supervisors if they would hire interns if an entry-level position were available. In summarizing outcomes, the school tabulated and reported results in four separate concentrations: broadcast sales promotion, broadcast news, public relations, and news editorial (Arizona State University, 2002–2003). The report indicated that 96% of interns were evaluated as being ready for an entry-level position. This impressive finding suggests that the Cronkite School provides students with the knowledge and skills needed for entering the profession. Similarly, a daily or weekly journal of activities might say something about a student's writing ability and describe the tasks a student was allowed to perform. But a better method might be a "guided entry" approach to writing a journal or final report. For example, the internship coordinator might ask interns to discuss their major duties and responsibilities, explain which courses helped prepare them for completing duties, or describe why they would or would not recommend an internship site to another student.

For the purposes of assessment, core competencies should be addressed, such as effective writing skills, speaking and presentation skills, production skills, and knowledge of the discipline and profession. Also, academic requirements must provide for an examination of more broadly defined learning objectives, such as "basic knowledge" and "basic skills," for journalism and communication disciplines, as enumerated by Turk (1997). A unit must decide what basic knowledge and skills need to be assessed.

Two types of records derived from internships seem appropriate for analysis: objective measures (data) and subjective measures (anecdotal evidence).

***Objective Measures.*** Units should maintain and report objective measures, such as the following:

- Number of students completing internships.
- Types of internships completed (by discipline and within disciplines).
- Location of internships (local, national, and international).

- Level and status of internship sites.
- Worksite supervisors' evaluation forms (evaluation criteria should reflect program goals and objectives).
- Internship assignment grades (portfolio, journal or diary, etc.).
- Internship final grades.

Although these data are useful in offering a "snapshot" of an internship program in a particular year, they also may be particularly insightful in showing trends in an academic program, for better or worse. Such objective measures provide a context for program administrators and accreditation organizations. For example, knowing the types of internships as related to majors might reveal changes in industry employment patterns. Knowing how many students were able to complete internships in national or international media markets may help gauge the ability of students to access media opportunity at the highest professional level.

**Subjective Measures.** In addition, academic units should use subjective measures, such as the following:

- Worksite supervisor comments.
- Daily or weekly journals or diaries.
- Reports or reflection papers.
- Notes from debriefing session with academic supervisor.

These subjective measures provide valuable anecdotal evidence in assessing an academic program. Evaluations completed by worksite supervisors, might offer valuable impressions about the abilities of students in terms of writing, critical thinking, and production skills. For example, interns and employers don't always agree on the value of knowledge and skills in an academic program. Hilt and Lipschultz (1999) found that although both interns and employers agreed with the statement, "College should teach students hands-on skills," they disagreed with the statement, "Students learn adequate hands-on skills in college" (p. 16). Although interns felt they had adequate hands-on skills, employers did not agree.

A clear methodology for analysis must be established when using such subjective measures. Graham, Bourland-Davis, and Fulmer (1997), for example, conducted a content analysis of midterm student reports to identify specific work tasks of public relations interns. One specific program outcome read as follows: "To offer students a program consistent with current public relations practices" (p. 202). To analyze this outcome, each internship task was compared to course descriptions or syllabi. The authors used the results to recommend content modifications to existing courses and to recommend the creation of a new course to address specific aspects of public relations writing. Similar content analytic studies could be conducted on student journals, calendars, or portfolios.

Table 17.1 identifies key program objectives that may relate to the items on an intern evaluation instrument. These objectives are based in part on ACEJMC values and competencies. Appendix A offers an example of an Intern Evaluation Form that attempts to relate specific items to program objectives. The Student Intern Evaluation Form is intended for illustrative purposes only. As an assessment tool, an academic unit may or may not use this instrument to address all program objectives. A pro-

TABLE 17.1
Internship Evaluation and Program Objectives (An Assessment Tool)[a]

| Objectives | Evaluation Question(s) |
|---|---|
| Values (ACEJMC) | |
| First Amendment principles and law | 10 |
| History and role of professionals and institutions in shaping communication | 11 |
| Diversity in a global society in relation to communications | 12 |
| Theories in use and presentations of images and information | 13 |
| Professional ethical principles in pursuit of truth, accuracy, fairness, and diversity | 14 |
| Competencies (ACEJMC) | |
| Think critically, creatively, and independently | 1, 2, 3 |
| Conduct research and evaluation information | 4 |
| Write correctly and clearly in forms and styles appropriate to communications professions | 5, 6 |
| Evaluate own and others work for accuracy and fairness, clarity, appropriate style, and grammatical correctness | 7 |
| Apply tools and technologies appropriate for communications professionals | 8 |
| Apply numerical and statistical concepts | 9 |
| Other (Departmental Objectives) | |
| Verbal (oral) and nonverbal presentation skills | 15 |
| Interpersonal communication skills | 16 |
| Reliability, punctuality, and attendance | 17 |
| Appearance, grooming, and appropriate attire | 18 |

*Note.* ACEJMC = Accrediting Council on Education in Journalism and Mass Communications.
[a]ACEJMC values and competencies and "other" department objectives are used as examples of program objectives that may be addressed by assessment. For convenience, these ACEJMC objectives have been categorized by the writer as "values" or "competencies." ACEJMC does not make this distinction.

gram may decide, for example, that the Student Intern Evaluation Form is useful for evaluating competencies, but another instrument, such as a guided entry journal or a reflection paper, is more appropriate for evaluating values.

The internship is one form of indirect measures for program assessment. As an assessment tool, internship data and anecdotal evidence should help reveal important trends and consistent or conflicting information and opinions.

## CAREERS

Employment is another indirect measure that may be useful in the assessment of an academic program. The ability of graduates to acquire entry-level positions in the field may prove useful in evaluating how well an academic unit achieves its goals and objectives. Similarly, consulting with employers can provide valuable information concerning how well a program's graduates are prepared for the workplace. Sometimes employers and graduates offer surprising opinions. As noted by Hilt and Lipschultz (1999), some employers express disappointment with the work quality of employees, their knowledge of the liberal arts, writing, and technological skills. Should an academic program receive similar responses from employers about its graduates, corrective actions (such as adjustments to course requirements or changes to specific courses) should be taken to improve curriculum and instruction.

Getting a job in the field is the ultimate goal for many students in journalism and mass communications. Some students change their minds late in their academic career, but many persist in their desire to work in the newspaper business, broadcasting, public relations, advertising, or in evolving careers, such as Web publishing. The future looks good, according to some observers of media careers and academic programs. A media career guide stated the following: "Despite economic forces increasing competition, most communication fields are growing, offering college graduates a wide variety of opportunities" (Seguin, 2002, p. 5). This optimistic view is supported by the results of a survey of BEA institutions that showed nearly 60% of students found employment in their field on graduation (Shriver, 2004).

Thus, it seems reasonable that using indirect external measures based on information received about the workplace from employers and graduates is an entirely appropriate way to assess the ability of students to successfully enter the profession. Although employment information is not necessarily a measure of student learning, it is yet another indirect "indicator" that learning has occurred.

## Implementation of Career Evaluations

Typically, information concerning employment is acquired by surveying graduates, employers, or both. Many academic units conduct their own surveys, or attach questions targeted to majors in more widely circulated university surveys. Please refer to the previous chapter for a more detailed discussion of surveys as an indirect measure of assessment.

This discussion focuses on using surveys to address questions specifically related to employment. Survey questions for employers might seek to ascertain information about the writing ability and production skills of graduates in entry-level positions, and evolving skill requirements in the workplace.

One example of using a survey of employers is the Newspaper Majors Program of the Grady College of Journalism and Mass Communication at the University of Georgia. Its assessment plan stated the following: "College surveys of employers will allow the Grady College to assess the effectiveness of the educational program as perceived by employers of recent graduates" (University of Georgia, 1996, p. 3). The employer survey is conducted in the second year of a 3-year assessment plan cycle. Survey questions for graduates might ask for an overall impression of the value of the educational experience as a major, what courses in the major were the most valuable in an entry-level job, or about the knowledge or skills that should be included in the curriculum.

In addition, a survey of graduates should provide descriptive information about the employment situation. For example, a report on a survey of graduates for the School of Journalism and Mass Communication at the University of Colorado at Boulder included average salary data, a comparison of current salaries with graduates 4 years earlier, a comparison of graduate salaries with national salaries, a rating of "preparation" by the School of Journalism and Mass Communication for their careers, and self-reported data on job "happiness" or "satisfaction." The survey also found "69% of the respondents working in journalism-related jobs eight months after graduation" (University of Colorado, 1999, p. 6).

Another way to use information related to the careers of graduates in assessment is to cite indicators of excellence in the workplace. For example, the Visual Communication program at Ohio University lists the success of one of its graduates in its assessment report: "The pinnacle of a professional journalism career is to win a Pulitzer Prize. This year's

Pulitzer Prize in spot news photography was awarded to a VisCom graduate . . ." (Ohio University, 2002, p. 6). Granted, this is a singular achievement; however, the magnitude of this award makes it an outstanding example or indicator of student learning.

## Careers As Assessment

An academic unit can learn a lot about itself by analyzing the employment of graduates. A program could learn more about the knowledge and skills that employers seek for entry-level positions, or that its curriculum leads a number of alumni into law school or graduate school, or gain insight into a rapidly changing job market. For example, using data from the Annual Survey of Journalism and Mass Communication Graduates, Lowrey and Becker (2001) found that "skill with presentation technologies matters to the job-finding success" of graduates (p. 766). Similarly, an academic program also might learn what skills are essential to job-finding, or how its graduates compare with graduates from other academic programs.

## COMPETITIONS

Student competitions are another indirect measure of assessment. According to ACEJMC (2001), "a unit's record over time of student entry and performance in contests may provide insight into student competence and into the effectiveness of curriculum, instruction and student learning" (p. 4). Competitions include contests, awards, scholarships, and fellowships, and publications and presentations of scholarly and creative works.

Competitions may be local, regional, national, or international. They may be sponsored by media companies, religious and professional organizations, universities, and foundations. Some competitions may offer cash awards, scholarships, or other tangible benefit. Others may simply acknowledge winners with a certificate. Competitions may be professional or academic. This distinction is usually reflected in the sponsoring organization.

Although not intended as a complete list, well-known professional competitions for students in journalism and mass communications include the following: the Hearst Journalism Awards Program (six writing, three photojournalism, two radio broadcast news, and two television broadcast news competitions each academic year), The Freedom Forum/NCAA Sports Journalism Scholarship Award, the Scripps Howard

Foundation "Top Ten" Student Scholarship Program, the Roy W. Howard National Reporting Competition, the Society of Professional Journalists (SPJ) Mark of Excellence (and other local and regional SPJ contests), National Broadcasting Society Student Electronic Media Competitions, Broadcast Education Association Student Competitions, Public Relations Student Society of America Awards (including the Award for Outstanding Public Relations Student, and the Bateman Case Study Competition), and the American Advertising Federation's (AAF) National Student Advertising Competition.

Academic competitions (scripts, articles, publications, productions, and presentations) also are impressive indicators for program assessment. Many journalism and mass communications programs define scholarship broadly based on the four categories of Ernest Boyer's framework (1990). As a result, numerous opportunities are available for students and graduates for research and creative activities, such as scriptwriting and screenplay competitions, video and film festivals, and submissions of academic papers to journals and conferences. Examples of these competitions include Association for Education in Journalism and Mass Communication (AEJMC) regional and national conferences, Broadcast Education Association, PRSSA, and the National Conference for Undergraduate Research. See Appendix B for a selected list of student competitions.

## Implementation of Competitions Evaluation

Undergraduate research has become important at many institutions. Papers and projects that are submitted for consideration often grow out of courses. These academic works often represent a considerable collaborative effort between a professor and student. As observed by Rodrick and Dickmeyer (1995), "undergraduate research provides a unique opportunity for faculty members to work in a personal setting with students. In this setting it is possible to motivate and encourage both the strongest and most marginal students so they achieve their fullest potential" (p. 42). Clearly, successful juried competition of papers, projects, and other creative works must be considered in evaluating the ability of a program to achieve its goals and objectives.

Some academic programs take a structured approach to encouraging student participation in competitions. For example, one goal of the Strategic Plan of the School of Mass Communication at Texas Tech University is to increase participation in national student academic competitions. Assessment of this goal is accomplished by an annual review of "the number of courses used and the number of students who participate in national student competitions" (Texas Tech University, n.d., p. 9).

Similarly, the Scripps School of Journalism at Ohio University has a designated faculty member who oversees entries in competitions. The success of this approach is evident in the School's assessment report which indicated that Scripps students have placed in the Hearst Journalism Awards in writing and broadcasting, a Top Ten scholarship winner in the Scripps Howard Top Ten Scholarship, and an SPJ Mark of Excellence Award for a student-produced magazine (Ohio University, Scripps).

Another example of this proactive approach to encouraging student competition is described in the 2003 to 2004 Assessment Plan for the Communication Department at Southern Utah University. The plan calls for student participation in the Forensics program as one way of achieving its goal to promote skills in oral presentation. This goal is to be assessed by "national team and individual rankings and success at tournaments" (Southern Utah University, 2003–2004, p. 2).

## Competitions as Assessment

Like internships and careers, competitions are indicators of student learning. Competitions are a valid form of assessment for three reasons: they involve some form of external review or evaluation of students or graduates, they provide a basis for peer comparison, and they connect the academic program to prestigious companies and organizations.

Both quantitative and qualitative indicators are used in assessing achievements in competitions. The School of Visual Communication at Ohio University reported the success of its students in several prestigious competitions as "indicators of excellence." Students won more awards in the College Photographer of the Year contest than any other school in the country, graduate students won awards in the Pictures of the Year professional photographer competition, and multiple awards in the Hearst Foundation Photojournalism Competition and numerous scholarships were received by students (Ohio University). Such awards and scholarships are yet another indication of recognition outside the academic unit.

## CONCLUSION

Three types of indirect measures are discussed in this chapter: internships, careers, and competitions. Appendix C outlines steps for programs that are interested in using indirect measures as part of an assessment plan.

Each of these external measures offers a unique opportunity to gauge the success or failure of an academic program. Internships as an indicator in assessment connect theory and practice. As suggested by Limburg (1994), an internship "is the practical application of the concepts, principles and skills learned in the classroom. It could also be considered the final test for a sound curriculum in preparing the student for a profession" (p. 182). Careers are a primary focus of many journalism and mass communications programs. The ability of graduates to succeed in job acquisition and performance reflects directly on the knowledge and skills offered by a program. As such, data solicited from graduates and employers give an academic program insight into what is valued and needed by the professions. Competitions as indicators in assessment illustrate the ability of students and graduates to compete in external environments. Professional and academic competitions enable students to demonstrate how they compare with peers through an external review process.

This chapter began with a discussion of the relation between the professional orientation of journalism and communications programs and indirect measures of assessment. Although this orientation is useful in evaluating student learning in a context beyond the classroom, the process, as assessment, is not without problems. First, each internship, employment, or competition situation is unique. The constraints and opportunities in different external environments may vary greatly. As a result, quantitative and subjective measures may not be comparable and the compilation of such information may be misleading. Second, external evaluators may have unrealistic expectations about the abilities of interns, entry-level employees, or students who enter competitions. Different evaluators may have very different estimations of competencies. As a consequence, evaluations may be anecdotal at best. Third, because not all students may be required to complete an internship, seek employment in a communication-related field, or enter competitions, participants may be self-selected. This may result in a small and potentially skewed sample of students. A small self-selected sample of specific cases may or may not be representative of a wider population of students in a program. Finally, internships, careers, and competitions may not address the acquisition of high-level knowledge. The focus of external environments may be more on doing than knowing. A program may decide that assessment of substantive areas, such as theory, history, social impact, and policy, may be better evaluated using direct measures.

As with all forms of assessment, indirect measures are meaningful only as related to core values and competencies addressed by an academic unit's curriculum. Journalism and mass communications programs should engage the indirect measures discussed in this chapter as sources of additional information, external validation, and indicators of how well they succeed in achieving goals and objectives.

# REFERENCES

Accrediting Council on Education in Journalism and Mass Communications. (2001). *A guide to assessment of student learning in journalism and mass communications.* Lawrence, KS: Author.

Accrediting Council on Education in Journalism and Mass Communications. (2003). Standards of accreditation (adopted September 2003). Lawrence, KS: Author.

Arizona State University, Cronkite School of Journalism and Mass Communication. (2002–2003). *Cronkite School: Learning outcome assessment.* Retrieved March 10, 2005, from http://129.219.216.161/assess/2003_2004/04Journalism.pdf

Astin, A. W. (1993). *Assessment for excellence: The philosophy and practice of assessment and evaluation in higher education.* New York: American Council on Education/Oryx Press.

Basow, R. R., & Byrne, M. V. (1993). Internship expectations and learning goals. *Journalism Educator, 47*(4), 48–54.

Beard, F., & Morton, L. (1999). Effects of internship predictors on successful field experience. *Journalism & Mass Communication Educator, 53,* 42–53.

Boyer, E. L. (1990). *Scholarship reconsidered: Priorities of the professoriate.* Princeton, NJ: Carnegie Foundation for the Advancement of Teaching.

Duhe, S. F., & Zukowski, L. A. (1997). Radio-TV journalism curriculum: First jobs and career preparation. *Journalism & Mass Communication Educator, 52,* 4–15.

Gibson, D. C. (1998). Public relations internship system evaluation: Criteria and a preliminary instrument. *Public Relations Review, 24*(1), 67–83.

Graham, B., Bourland-Davis, P., & Fulmer, H. (1997). Using the internship as a tool for assessment: A case study. *Journal of the Association of Communication Administration, 3,* 198–205.

Gross, L. (1981). *The internship experience.* Prospect Heights, IL: Waveland.

Hilt, M. L., & Lipschultz, J. H. (1999). Comparing views of broadcasters and student interns about career preparation. *Feedback, 40*(4), 14–19.

Katula, R., & Threnhauser, E. (1999). Experiential education in the undergraduate curriculum. *Communication Education, 48,* 238–255.

Limburg, V. E. (1994). Internships, exit interviews, and advisory boards. In W. G. Christ (Ed.), *Assessing communication education: A handbook for media, speech and theatre educators* (pp. 181–200). Hillsdale, NJ: Lawrence Erlbaum Associates, Inc.

Lowrey, W., & Becker, L. B. (2001). The impact of technological skill on job-finding success in the mass communication labor market. *Journalism & Mass Communication Quarterly, 78,* 754–770.

Ohio University, E. W. Scripps School of Journalism. (2002). *Assessment report.* Retrieved February 19, 2004, from http://www.ohioedu/provost/SLOA2001_2002/journalism2002b.doc.

Ohio University, School of Visual Communication. (1997–1998). *1997–98 VisCom assessment report*. Retrieved February 19, 2004, from http://www.ohiou.edu/instres/assessments/97_98assess/dept/viscom.htm

Public Relations Student Society of America. (n.d.). *Establish a new chapter*. Retrieved February 9, 2004, from http://www.prssa.org/about/establish.asp.

Rodrick, R., & Dickmeyer, L. (1995). Providing undergraduate research opportunities for communication students: A curricular approach. *Communication Education, 51*, 40–50.

Shriver, R. (2004). A look at current trends in media education in the U.S. *Feedback, 45*(1), 7–13.

Seguin, J. (2002). *Media career guide: Preparing for jobs in the 21st century* (3rd ed.). New York: Bedford/St. Martin's.

Southern Utah University, Communication Department. (2003–2004). *Assessment plan and report*. Retrieved March 11, 2005, from http://www.suu.edu/general/ir/0304/comm-plan.pdf

Texas Tech University. (n.d.). *School of Mass Communications strategic plan*. Retrieved March 11, 2005, from http://www.depts.ttu.edu/mcom/reports/mccomstrategicplan.pdf

Turk, J. V. (1997). Journalism and mass communication programs. In W. G. Christ (Ed.), *Media education assessment handbook* (pp. 79–98). Mahwah, NJ: Lawrence Erlbaum Associates, Inc.

University of Colorado at Boulder, Office of Planning, Budget, and Analysis. School of Journalism and Mass Communication. Last updated 6/15/1999. Retrieved March 11, 2005, from http://www.colorado.edu/pba/outcomes/units/jour.htm

University of Georgia, College of Journalism and Mass Communication, Newspaper Majors. (1996). *Assessment plan for the department of journalism*. Retrieved March 11, 2005, from http://www.uga.edu/ovpi/program_review/committee/reports/0203/news0203.pdf

Whitlow, S. (2003). The internship program. In M. Murray & R. Moore (Eds.), *Mass communication education* (pp. 339–357). Ames: Iowa State University Press.

# APPENDIX A

## Student Intern Evaluation Form

Student _____ Internship Period: From _____ To _____ Hrs. Worked
Company/Organization _____ Location_____
Supervisor _____ Title _____

Directions: Please evaluation the student intern from 1 (strongly agree) to 5 (strongly disagree) or NA (not applicable to the work environment or internship) on each of the items below. Comments are helpful.

1. Ability to work independently in completing task     1  2  3  4  5  NA
Comments: _____

2. Shows creative potential in completing work assignments    1  2  3  4  5  NA
Comments: _____

3. Ability to analyze, solve problems and think critically    1   2   3   4   5   NA
Comments: _____

4. Research and information seeking skills    1   2   3   4   5   NA
Comments: _____

5. Clear, correct and appropriate writing style    1   2   3   4   5   NA
Comments: _____

6. Knowledgeable of script style and formats    1   2   3   4   5   NA
Comments: _____

7. Ability to evaluate the work of self and others    1   2   3   4   5   NA
Comments: _____

8. Knowledgeable of and the ability to use computer
applications and equipment    1   2   3   4   5   NA
Comments: _____

9. Ability to use basic numerical and statistical concepts    1   2   3   4   5   NA
Comments: _____

10. Understanding of laws, regulations and issues that
pertain to work environment    1   2   3   4   5   NA
Comments: _____

11. Knowledge of the well known individuals, history and
issues pertaining to the profession    1   2   3   4   5   NA
Comments: _____

12. Shows awareness of diversity in the workplace and in
the creation of communication content    1   2   3   4   5   NA
Comments: _____

13. Understanding of theoretical concepts related to the
presentation of images and information (such as,

composition of images, persuasive appeals, influence
of message on audience and society, etc.)              1  2  3  4  5   NA
Comments: _____

14. Appropriate ethical behavior for the professional
    workplace                                          1  2  3  4  5   NA
Comments: _____

15. Demonstrates clear and appropriate verbal (oral)
    and nonverbal presentation skills                  1  2  3  4  5   NA
Comments: _____

16. Demonstrates good interpersonal communication skills
    (works well to achieve group tasks)                1  2  3  4  5   NA
Comments: _____

17. Reliability, punctuality and attendance            1  2  3  4  5   NA
Comments: _____

18. Appearance, grooming and attire appropriate for the
    workplace                                          1  2  3  4  5   NA
Comments: _____

19. Greatest strengths

_____
_____

20. Greatest weaknesses

_____
_____

21. Overall evaluation. (Please recommend a grade for
    the work done by our intern.)                      1  2  3  4  5   NA
Comments: _____

22. Would you recommend this intern for a permanent
    position at your company or organization?
    _____ Yes      _____ No

Signature _____   Title _____   Date_____

## APPENDIX B

### Selected Student Competitions' Web Sites

The American Advertising Federation's (AAF) National Student Advertising Competition: http://www.aaf.org/college/nsac.html

Academy of Television Arts & Sciences Foundation (ATAS): http://www.emmys.org/foundation/collegetvawards.php

Academy of Motion Picture Arts and Sciences Student Awards: http://www.oscars.org/saa

Association for Education in Journalism and Mass Communication: http://www.aejmc.org

Broadcast Education Association Student Competitions: http://www.beafestival.org/student.html

Columbia Scholastic Press Association (Gold Circle and Gold Crown Awards): http://www.columbia.edu/cu/cspa/

Hearst Journalism Awards Program: http://www.hearstfdn.org/hearst_journalism

The Freedom Forum/NCAA Sports Journalism Scholarship Award (NCAA Foundation Web site): http://www.ncaa.org/leadership_advisory_board/programs.html

National Association of Television Program Executives (NATPE) Student Production Contest: http://www.natpe.org/about/educational/student.shtml

National Broadcasting Society (NBS/AERho) Student Electronic Media Competitions (Ohio Northern University Web site): http://www.onu.edu/org/nbs/StudentProdApp.doc

National Conference for Undergraduate Research (NCUR): http://www.ncur.org

Public Relations Student Society of America: http://www.prssa.org/resources/MemberAwards.asp

Roy W. Howard National Reporting Competition: http://www.scripps.com/foundation/programs/rwhcomp/rwhcomp.html

Scripps Howard Foundation "Top Ten" Student Scholarship Program: http://www.scripps.com/foundation/programs/program.html

Society of Professional Journalists Mark of Excellence: http://www.spj.org/awards_moe.asp

## APPENDIX C

### Steps for Using Indirect Measures in an Assessment Plan

1. Identify key program objectives (may be linked to Accrediting Council on Education in Journalism and Mass Communications values and competencies).
2. Identify where and how key objectives are addressed in the academic program (goals or objectives of specific courses in the curriculum, required workshops and extracurricular activities, etc.).
3. Identify the specific objective and subjective measures that will be used to evaluate each program objective in Step 1:
   A. Internships (work-site supervisor evaluation; portfolio; journal and diaries, etc.).
   B. Careers (work-site supervisor or graduate surveys, numerical employment data, etc.).
   C. Competitions (numerical evidence of submissions and winners of contests, awards, scholarships, and fellowships, and publications and presentations of scholarly and creative works).
4. Establish clear methodologies for the evaluation of measures used in Step 3.
5. Establish guidelines for how a program will gauge the success or failure of findings (for example, is 60% employment in a communications-related field a year after graduation an indication of success or failure?).
6. Summarize, interpret, and report results (compare findings with objectives in Step 1 and guidelines in Step 5 to gauge success or failure).
7. Implement changes based on results.

# Direct Measures: Examinations

David E. Tucker
*Department of Communication*
*University of Toledo*

Assessment: It is the systematic collection, review, and use of information about educational programs undertaken for the purpose of improving student learning and development (Palomba & Banta, 1999). Depending on age, departmental structure, state in which one resides, or personal belief, a faculty member's view toward the topic of assessment varies dramatically. Opinions abound. They run a continuum from "assessment is important" to "our very existence" to "it's a complete waste of time" (Barrington, 2003). But, whatever your position, it has been rendered essentially irrelevant. Faculty no longer have a choice about whether to do assessment. The regional accrediting associations now demand direct assessment of student performance. Moore (1992) said direct assessment techniques should provide the department with evidence that student learning, in the form of student outcomes, has really taken place. Outcomes may include the following: knowledge, understanding, application, thinking skills, general skills, attitudes, interests, appreciation. Assessment asks the following:

1. What should graduates of a specific program know, be able to do, and value?
2. Have these graduates acquired this learning?
3. How can student learning be improved?

Accrediting agencies also make it clear what assessment is not: it is not a faculty evaluation or a comprehensive program review. In addition, it does not have to be "high stakes" testing where students will fail to graduate if they fail whatever assessment procedure the department has chosen. It is, rather, an effort to improve teaching and learning by measuring student outcomes. According to the North Central Association, one of the regional agencies, a properly functioning assessment program will allow faculty members to ". . . routinely link their assessment findings to decision making and instructional and program improvement" (Higher Learning Commission/North Central Association, 2002, p. 21) On the surface, it appears to be a laudable goal that should be relatively simple to achieve. However, depending on a variety of factors, it may not be a "simple" process.

Objective exams, oral exams, performance assessments, surveys, and a capstone experience are all direct measures of student outcomes. This chapter will look at the exit exam as a method of direct assessment. Exit exams are most utilized at the elementary and secondary levels. This is generally "high-stakes" testing where the student is allowed to move up a grade or graduate from high school based on a score or set of scores received. Schools and school systems receive funding based on student scores. The scores are compared to other schools and school districts across the state and country. Developed at the state or national level, the tests cover specific material deemed by state or federal officials as important for students at that particular level. Such "high-stakes" testing is also utilized by some states (Tennessee and South Dakota among them) to measure how well their colleges and universities are doing. And, as with elementary and secondary education, funding and other resources are tied to the results (Rylander, 2000).

Such testing at the level of higher education may seem uncommon, but actually has been prevalent in teacher education and professional schools (pharmacy, engineering, business, and architecture) for a long time. At the entry level, high-stakes testing is often used in communication departments. Grammar tests are used by journalism programs for entry into basic news writing. Programs require students to pass the basic speech course or gain a "C or better" in basic classes before allowing them to continue with the program. Scholastic Assessment Test (SAT) and American College Testing (ACT) scores are used for entry into some majors. Masters and PhD programs give comprehensive exams that are essentially exit exams. So the idea of testing for achievement, or possible future achievement, is not new, even in mass communication. The movement toward the use of an exit exam seems to be waxing, not waning. A cursory Yahoo search using "exit exam + mass communication" rendered, in the first five pages, over 30 programs using exit exams in some form. So, for those faculty who believe assessment and testing will somehow disappear, the trend is not in their favor.

Some disciplines have an advantage in the area of exit exams. There is an agreed-on body of knowledge that can be tested. Curricula have been developed over the years that address this knowledge and it is fairly easy to test a student to see if he or she knows what he or she is supposed to know. For instance, the Graduate Record Exam will test students in eight different areas: Biochemistry, Biology, Chemistry, Computer Science, Literature in English, Mathematics, Physics, and Psychology. There is no Graduate Record Exam for Communication, Mass Communication, or Broadcasting. The National Communication Association (NCA) has no such exam and neither does the Broadcast Education Association (BEA) or the Association for Education in Journalism and Mass Communication (AEJMC). The argument is that communication programs differ to such a degree that no national, comprehensive exam is possible. Programs vary from the very specific (television production) to umbrella programs that require courses in a variety of areas (public speaking, mass communication, and communication theory). Therefore, it is probably true that creating a "one-size-fits-all" test would be difficult. However, it should be noted that NCA has been active in creating communication competencies for high school students. NCA also has a significant body of assessment material on its Web site (http://www.natcom.org/), including "Criteria for Assessment of Oral Communication" and "Expected Student Outcomes for Speaking and Listening." Therefore, it may be possible to agree on a set of learning outcomes for specific areas and hence create national exams by area. The idea is further explored later in the chapter.

## GENERAL TESTING ISSUES

There are some general issues regarding the use of exit exams or testing for assessment purposes that should be addressed. First, it is necessary to ask what good exams do. Dietel, Herman, and Knuth (1991) gave the following as good characteristics of a classroom test:

1. The content of the tests should match the classroom objectives and what the teacher emphasized.
2. The test items should represent the full range of knowledge and skills that are the primary targets of instruction.
3. Expectations for student performance should be clear.
4. The assessment should be free of extraneous factors, which unnecessarily confuse or inadvertently cue student responses. (pp. 2–3)

Although they were discussing in-class testing, there is no reason to assume an exit exam is anything except a large in-class test. The content of the exam must match all the learning objectives and outcomes the department has listed. The test should match in its emphasis the curriculum taken by the individual student. This is just not easy to do, not even when students have taken the same classes. For example, there are many ways to teach Mass Communication and Society. It can be done chronologically. It can be done using issues. It can be done in segments (history, regulation, etc.). It can be done by industry (radio, print, television, film, etc.). There are 16 weeks in a semester and approximately 3 years worth of material that might be covered. Different people teach the class at most universities. Although teachers can agree on the class objectives, all may take different roads to get there. The construction of a test that adequately examines these issues becomes a challenge. It might be possible for a media unit to specify content and methodology, but that then raises the issue of academic freedom.

## Experimental Design

An exit exam is essentially an experiment. The department has applied its treatment (the curriculum) to an experimental group (the students) and is now measuring (the exit exam) to determine if the treatment "worked." Campbell and Stanley (1963) noted that studies in which a single group is studied only once (in this case the single exit exam), "have such a total absence of control as to have no scientific value" (p. 6). They also noted, for those departments using a pretest, that the single group pretest–posttest design is almost as worthless. There are significant intervening variables that play havoc with the results. Among those are history, maturation, testing, instrumentation, regression, selection, mortality, and various forms of interaction among these variables. In other words, the data derived from such exams have no validity. They are not generalizable in the sense that the data only speak to one group. The data are, at the very least, worthless, and in some cases, they may be injurious to the department, leading the department in the wrong direction. Campbell and Stanley recommended a pretest–posttest design with a control group. Such a requirement would put extraordinary pressures on an academic department. Using a pretest essentially doubles the department's workload. Using a control would double it again. Using a pretest–posttest design with a control group also exacerbates some of the problems encountered when using single exit exams. Security, time, money, curriculum, faculty, and so on are all issues that are discussed later in this chapter. And, unless participation becomes mandatory, randomization and representation become major issues as well.

Citing a specific case from the Advertising Department of The University of Tennessee at Knoxville, Haley and Jackson (1995) pointed out that rapidly changing areas such as mass communication and advertising make a longitudinal test essentially worthless. They also pointed to the validity problems of testing only one group. Unless the test only covers material the student could have learned in the department, there is no way of knowing where it was learned. Campbell and Stanley (1963) would state that without a control group, even if you believe you are testing only information given in your department's classes, you will have no way of knowing that to be true.

## Learning

The exit exam is designed to measure learning. Somehow the department is supposed to be able say, "this is what we taught, and this is what they learned." How simple or how complex the measurement of learning becomes depends to a great deal on how the department defines learning. If learning is treated as an accumulation of facts, then an objective exam is useful. If learning is treated as integrated knowledge, then an essay exam is possible. If, however, learning is seen as a complex interaction among a variety of variables, then an exam is not likely to render relevant data. The American Association for Higher Education, the American College Personnel Association, and the National Association of Student Personnel Administrators (1988), in their report, *Powerful Partnerships: A Shared Responsibility for Learning,* developed 10 principles about learning. Although it is not the purpose of this chapter to reiterate those 10 principles, a few comments about the report are warranted. First, the report makes clear that learning is the responsibility of three segments of higher education—faculty, staff, and students. Any exam measuring only a small portion of one of those elements is going to be painfully inadequate. Second, when reading the principles themselves, one begins to understand the myriad issues involved in learning. For example, Principle Number Four stated the following: "Learning is developmental, a cumulative process involving the whole person, relating past and present, integrating the new with the old, starting from but transcending personal concerns and interests" (p. 6). The report went on to say that any assessment of learning should encompass all aspects of the educational experience. Again, any exam claiming to measure such learning will be inadequate.

## CONSIDERATIONS BEFORE CREATING THE EXIT EXAM

Given the lack of nationally normed exams in the area of mass communication, any department that decides to use an exit exam as a measure of direct assessment will have to create one. There are several issues that need to be considered before sitting down to write the exam. They include the following: the nature of the department, the number of full-time faculty, departmental requirements, curricular options, number of majors graduating each semester or year, uses to which the exam results will be put, money available for the development and administering of the exam and, the type(s) of exam(s) to be used. Several of these areas overlap, but are listed here separately because they all address the use of an exit exam in slightly different ways.

### Learning Outcomes

The very first step a department must take is the creation of learning outcomes and objectives for the curriculum as a whole. The faculty must know what knowledge or skills set they claim to be testing. The faculty must be able to explain to students what students must know or be able to do as the result of having been a mass communication major. An exit exam purports to measure those learning objectives. It is at this point that the nature of the department becomes relevant. Depending on the makeup of the department, the learning outcomes and objectives may be wide-ranging or fairly short. For instance, in a department of mass communication, a learning outcome or objective might be, "The student will exhibit an understanding of mass communication regulation." In a department of interpersonal and public communication, a learning outcome or objective might be, "The student will employ language appropriate to the designated audience." But, a department containing both disciplines might easily have both learning outcomes and objectives and hence have to test for both. If your department does not have a list of learning outcomes and objectives for graduating seniors, then it must develop one before attempting to write an exit examination or carry on any assessment at all.

The departmental learning outcomes should derive from the classes. Each class syllabus should have a list of learning outcomes. Each syllabus should also have a description of how students will be evaluated to see if they have achieved these outcomes, with each assignment specifically stating which outcomes are being tested. From the learning outcomes of the various classes, the department should be able to create a list of departmental learning outcomes and hence a list of those things the faculty have agreed on as necessary for their graduates. If, for some reason, the class syllabi do not have learning objectives and outcomes listed, then the faculty will have to start with each individual class.

## Curricular Issues

Although the curricular makeup of the department will determine the number of learning outcomes, it may also affect the number of exit exams. If the department has specific concentrations (electronic media, journalism, public relations, etc.), then an exam for each concentration might be necessary. If the department has a common core, then an exam covering the core classes is also a possibility. The more complicated the department's curricular requirements, the more complicated the exam(s).

## Full-Time Faculty

The number of full-time faculty will also play a role in determining whether to use an exit exam or some other form of direct student outcome measurement. If you have few full-time faculty and a large number of graduates, an exit exam might be very appealing—particularly an objective one. This issue goes to faculty time and the uses to which the evaluation will be put. The amount of faculty time invested in the exam may be directly related to the stakes involved. Being quite frank here, if resources are going to be allocated based on the quality of the assessment, then faculty should spend a great deal of time with whatever procedure is chosen. If, however, the faculty are doing assessment because an accrediting agency now requires it, and it will have no bearing on resources, then the faculty will probably choose the path of least resistance. On the surface, the exit exam seems to provide such a path. Be careful. First, a high-quality exit exam will not be easy to create. Second, if the department creates an exam because it seemed easy and the exam does not measure adequately student outcomes, either the accrediting agency or future administrations may hold the faculty accountable.

## Departmental Requirements

Departmental requirements also play a role in the development of an exam. As it implies, an exit exam is taken shortly before graduation. However, many departmental requirements may be taken early in the collegiate career. This is especially true of core classes that act as prerequisites to other upper-level classes. The department will find itself testing students on material taken several years earlier. If this material has been reinforced as the student has gone through the program, this will not be a problem. If, however, it has been 5 or 6 years since the student has been exposed to the material, then review sessions might be required. An even bigger issue is content in multiple section classes. To get an accurate reading on student learning, those classes have to be comparable. The learning outcomes need to be the same and the classes should have similar content.

The problem of concentrations in an umbrella department was mentioned earlier. But it is not just developing a test for each concentration, but how much variance there is within the concentration. If all students within a concentration are taking the same set of classes, then they will all be tested over similar material. If students can pick and choose within a concentration, then testing becomes significantly more difficult. Yet another issue surrounding the curriculum has to do with related or cognate areas. Some cognate areas may contribute more toward the student's ability to do well on an exit exam.

## Number of Majors

The number of majors will play a role in how the department decides to measure student outcomes. If the department has 2 full-time faculty and 10 students graduating per year, there are a number of options available, including combinations of measurement techniques. Essay exit exams, public presentations of research projects, portfolios, and internships are all possibilities. If the department has 8 full-time faculty and over 100 graduates per year, then time becomes a major issue no matter the measurement form. All forms of assessment are going to require an investment in time. For example, if the department decides on a portfolio (discussed in detail in another chapter), then either the student or the department will have to keep track of all the items to be brought forth at the time the portfolio is evaluated. If the department decides to evaluate writing assignments, the same problem is present. Likewise, time will be an issue in the creation and grading of exit exams if such exams are to be useful in assessment procedures. Therefore, the choice of one method over another should not be dependent on the amount of time faculty believe will have to be invested in the project on an annual basis. Although some methods may seem to be more time consuming than other methods, this is probably not true.

## Use of the Exit Exam

How the results of the exit exam will be used is another consideration. Accrediting agencies want the results to be used to improve teaching and learning. The goal is to see where your students are succeeding and where they are not. In those areas where students are not doing well, perhaps curricular or instructional changes can be made to improve student achievement. Although the agencies are, at this point, fairly benign and somewhat noble in their expectations, some states and administrations are not. Funding is tied to assessment and exit exams in Tennessee and South Dakota (Rylander, 2000) and is being considered in Texas and Florida. The very nature of an exit exam means there will be some number associated with the results. The expectation will then be that such a number rises each year. When the stakes are significant, as in funding, faculty lines, merit pay, or even the existence of the department, it requires both an ethically strong faculty and a commitment of resources to create and administer the exam.

## Capstone Class

Monetary resources are also an issue when deciding to use an exit exam. There will be costs involved in the creation, administration, and grading of any exam. If it is not a "high-stakes" exam, it may be necessary to provide an incentive for students to even take it. Incentives may also be necessary to get the students to take the exam seriously. These problems can be partially avoided if the exam becomes a part of a regularly graded class, such as a capstone class. A capstone class combines the idea of an exit exam with that of a regular course and is fully discussed in another chapter. The course should, through its various assignments, require students to draw on their curricular experiences and exhibit the student outcomes listed by the faculty as necessary for graduation. The capstone instructor then places students at the level the instructor believes they have obtained on any particular outcome listed by the faculty. There are several drawbacks. Unless the class is team-taught, one faculty member is doing the assessment work for the entire department, and conclusions drawn from the class might vary dramatically depending on who is teaching the class. In addition, the assignments must truly reflect student outcomes as defined by the faculty. This essentially means the entire faculty must agree on the assignments for the capstone class. There will also be the problem of having one class evaluate anywhere from 8 to 20 student learning objectives and outcomes. Assume the department using the capstone class is an umbrella department and has as two of its learning outcomes "the student will exhibit the ability to persuade others in a public setting," and, "the student will be able to apply mass communication theory in everyday settings." The first issue is whether the faculty member teaching the class is qualified to judge both of those objectives. The second issue is curricular. Everyone in the class may not have taken the same classes, and third, the work on one assignment is now substituting for an entire semester's work in a previous class.

## Other Issues

There are other items that must be considered by a department before going through the process of creating an exit exam. Security is an issue. This is not just a problem when the students are taking the exam. Care must be taken in guarding the questions, the answer sheet, and the final grades on the exam. There is also the problem of students taking the exam late. Someone will have been hospitalized or their father will have died (ask for an obituary) and the department will have to allow for that. The department will have to create a second exam. This exam will have to be similar in nature to the first. There will also be the necessity of keeping the results of the exams separate to determine if students benefited by taking the exam late. When exams are given each year or each semester, different questions have to be devised. Students who take the exam one year will talk to those who have yet to take the exam. Such student interaction will affect the test scores and hence the usefulness of the exam as an assessment tool. Changing the exam significantly from semester to semester or year to year raises questions of reliability and validity as well.

The department will have to address all of these questions and issues before deciding whether to use an exit exam or some other form of assessment. In an effort to show the process at work, let us look at a real-life example.

The Department of Communication at the University of Toledo is an umbrella department with approximately 600 majors and 10 full-time faculty. Courses are taught in communication, mass communication, public relations, and journalism. One hundred to 125 students per year graduate with a Communication Major. The curriculum was converged in 1997 and the Department of Communication no longer has concentrations. Instead, there are five core classes which include the following: Mass Communication and Society, Information Analysis and Synthesis, Public Presentations, Communication Theory, and a 1-hour Senior Portfolio. Students then evenly divide the rest of their course selections between Applied and Conceptual Communication. The maximum allowed in Communication is 43 semester hr. As of September 2003, the Department of Communication had a Mission Statement and each class had learning objectives and outcomes. It was thought that assessment was being handled by a survey given to graduating seniors that asked for their impressions of the curriculum, the department, and the faculty. The Department of Communication was informed that such a survey constituted indirect assessment and that some form of direct assessment was necessary. Because "high-stakes" testing has not yet come to Ohio's state universities, the faculty began to address options. One of those was to use an exit exam. Because the Department of Communication did not yet have learning outcomes for the entire curriculum, it was believed that an exam covering the core classes might be worth doing. The Department of Communication had the following learning outcomes for the core classes:

1. The student will exhibit competency in public communication both written and verbal.
2. The student will exhibit competency in problem solving.
3. The student will exhibit an understanding of mass communication and its relationship to both the individual and society.
4. The student will exhibit the ability to both find and differentiate among information sources.
5. The student will exhibit an understanding of the law and how it affects communication.
6. The student will exhibit the ability to apply communication theory to everyday problems.
7. The student will exhibit an understanding of social science theory. (Department of Communication, 2004a, p. 1)

The Department of Communication was hopeful that an objective exam given twice per year would suffice for assessment purposes. As we began working our way through the issues listed earlier, it became painfully obvious that an exit exam was not really an option. The creation of an exam covering adequately the aforementioned learning outcomes, particularly in an objective form, was not possible. The learning outcome listing both verbal and written competency ended that pretty quickly. Essay exams were discussed but entailed the same problem as the objective test in terms of verbal and written expression. Essay tests had added problems as well. There was the problem of creating enough high-quality questions to adequately get at the learning objectives, but the faculty believed that could be overcome. It was the grading of multiple essay questions for over 100 students a year that was going to be problematic. Blind grading of the essays would have to be used, thus creating a bookkeeping nightmare. Each essay would have to be given a number and then copied twice. Then, at least two professors would have to grade each question and there would have to be at least two questions for each core class. That turned out to be 8 essays for each student times 100 students. Just doing the math made the faculty tired. The cost in time alone was going to be significant. And, such a test was only going to cover the core classes. There was also the added problem of scheduling the test. One of the core classes is Communication Theory. Students do not generally take the class until their senior year, with some taking it the last semester of their senior year. The Department of Communication would, in a sense, be testing those students on material not yet covered while testing other students on material covered years earlier. Finally, because the test has no bearing on their graduation, the Department was going to have compliance problems. And, even if the students were required to take the exam, would they take it seriously enough to help with the Department's assessment issues? In other words, after all this work, the Department might have technically met its assessment requirement, but not have learned anything worth knowing. After lengthy discussions, the Department has opted for a modified portfolio methodology and reworked its learning outcomes.

## DEVELOPING THE EXIT EXAM

### Determining the Testing Method

Before determining the testing method it is suggested the department read two texts. The first was written by American Educational Research, the American Psychological Association, and the National Council on Measurement in Education (1999), and is titled, *Standards for Educational and Psychological Testing*. This text discussed test construction, evaluation, documentation, fairness, and application of national or departmental-wide evaluative tests. The second is *The Student Evaluation Standards* (Joint Commission on Standards for Educational Evaluation, 2003), which examines in-class evaluation procedures for propriety, utility, feasibility, and accuracy. Please understand, entire texts have been written on educational testing and entire classes, and in some cases, an entire series of classes, have been taught on the subject. There is a distinct possibility that few of us teaching college-level mass communication have been exposed to such classes. Use some outside expertise.

Assuming all of what has been discussed here takes place, a department must then determine what type, or types, of tests it's going to use. There are objective exams, essay exams, and combination exams. There are available national tests for writing and critical thinking from both Educational Testing Service (ETS) and ACT. If the department has learning outcomes that include written expression or problem solving, this may be an answer. The results will supply the department with nationally normed information about their students. Neither ETS nor ACT has Field Exams in Communication, Mass Communication, Electronic Communication, or Broadcasting. This means the department will have to create and grade any exam in these areas. The simplest to grade is the multiple-choice exam. It is blind grading as the computer does all or most of the work. The computer can give statistical breakouts on which questions are missed most often. The exam can be arranged by learning outcomes so that questions pertaining to particular outcomes can be easily broken out and examined. For assessment purposes, it is easy to determine which information students are learning and which information they have not retained. Haladyna (1999) claimed it is a misconception that such tests can only be used for factual recall. He believed that multiple-choice tests are best at measuring knowledge and do a fairly good job at measuring cognitive ability. Rodriguez (2002) said that multiple-choice tests can assess many skills, including the following: the ability to discriminate, understand concepts and principles, judge possible courses of action, infer, reason, complete statements, interpret data, and apply information. Koons (2000) believed that they can be structured to even measure critical thinking skills. He pointed to SAT-type tests wherein the student reads a passage and then is quizzed about the passage. On the surface, it appears to be a legitimate option for use in assessing a department's ability to teach. Some, however, believe that the objective exam does not get at real learning. Dietel, Herman, and Knuth (1991) discussed meaningful learning as

> ... reflective, constructive, and self-regulated. People are seen not as mere recorders of factual information but as creators of their own unique knowledge structures. To know something is not just to have received information but to have interpreted it and related it to other knowledge one already has. In addition, we now recognize the importance of knowing not just how to perform, but also when to perform and how to adapt the performance to new situations. Thus, the presence or absence of discrete bits of information—which is typically the focus of traditional multiple-choice tests—is not of primary importance in the assessment of meaningful learning. Rather, what is important is how and whether students organize, structure, and use that information in context to solve complex problems. (p. 4)

Davey and Neil (1994) claimed that the multiple-choice test does not "assess higher order thinking, problem solving abilities, creativity or initiative" (p. 2). Haladyna (1999) countered that the problem is that the definitions of critical thinking, problem solving, and creativity are often fluid and therefore difficult to test under any circumstances. He went on to point out that the test giver never really knows the process the test taker uses to answer a problem. The more expert one is in an area, the more likely rote memory can be used to solve a problem. That's because the expert has seen the problem before as opposed to the novice who may have to use critical thinking skills because he or she has never experienced the problem. Regardless of which side, pro or con, a researcher falls on, they all tend to agree that authoring a quality multiple-choice test is extremely difficult. If a department opts for an objective exam there are resources to help develop good questions (Frary, 1999; Kehoe, 1999; Osterlind, 1998).

The essay exam is a second option. The exam gives the department the ability to ask complex questions and gives students the opportunity to, in written form, show their ability to combine and draw on significant amounts of information. Depending on the number of students graduating, this might be a reasonable option. As with objective exams, there are the problems of developing questions, and then matching the questions to the classes taken and the learning outcomes that students should have obtained. The department will have to determine if grading will include grammar, punctuation, and spelling, in addition to content. A timed exam also measures the ability to recall information rapidly, so the department will have to determine how long students should have to complete it. The actual grading of the exam is problematic as well. If all the graders are doing is looking for specific words or phrases, then the essay exam is really an objective exam in disguise. With essay exams, there is also the issue of intergrader reliability. Each faculty member has to grade in a similar manner. This is why at least two faculty have to grade each essay. As was noted earlier, double blind grading will have to be instituted. In small departments, this probably will not insure anonymity for either the faculty grader or student. If only eight or nine students graduate each year, it is very likely that each professor will recognize which student has written which essay. Using essay exams in high-stakes testing also presents the problem of what constitutes passing and how that was measured. Assume the department has designated 70% as passing and one student receives 70% and passes, whereas a second student receives 69% and fails. The department will have to be able to defend its grading when the student who does not pass asks the department to explain the difference.

In the case of essay exams, the utilization of scoring rubrics is suggested (Moskal, 2002; Moskal & Leydens, 2002). A scoring rubric is a descriptive methodology used when a judgment of quality is involved. The faculty develop a predefined scheme as to what will be evaluated. So, in an exit exam setting, the faculty might set up the following categories: Failing, Barely Passing, Passing, and Passing with Honors. Under each category will be a list of statements describing the category and relating it to the specific question. It is possible to ascribe numeric weights to each statement in a category. In this way, grammar and punctuation might be considered but given less weight than content areas when evaluating the answer.

Moskal (2002) noted several steps involved in developing a scoring rubric. First, clearly identify the qualities that need to be displayed in the essay. Begin with those qualities that will exemplify the top category. Then develop criteria for the lowest category. After having decided what is, to use the aforementioned example, Passing with Honors, and what is Failing, then the intermediate categories should be fairly easy to derive. She suggested that the categories themselves be written as quantifiable. So instead of saying, "the student's understanding of broadcast regulation was good," the rubric will say, "the student made no false statements about broadcast regulation." Rubrics are available on-line for a wide variety of subjects. A web search is recommended.

As with learning outcomes, scoring rubrics should start with individual assignments. They should then be developed for each class based on the learning outcomes for the class and finally for the department. At the departmental level, the learning outcomes are listed down one side, whereas across the top are four levels of understanding. The department can title these levels anything it believes appropriate. Mansilla and Gardner (1998) labeled them as follows: Nothing, Naïve Understanding, Novice Understanding, Apprentice Understanding, and Master Understanding. Under each heading are given the abilities students must display to achieve that particular level. For instance, the Department of Communication at the University of Toledo has as one of its learning outcomes, "The student will exhibit the ability to appropriately explain or package a concept or message directed to a specified audience and/ or situation" (Department of Communication, 2004b, p. 1). This outcome is listed down the left-hand side of the page along with the other departmental outcomes. Across the top of the page are listed Mansilla and Gardner's five categories (see Appendix A). Under each category are the requirements necessary for students to reach that level. Using the rubric as a guide, assessment procedures should be able to place students into one of these categories. This will be almost impossible if the department uses an objective exam. It will be possible using an essay exam that is itself graded using scoring rubrics.

## THE NATIONAL EXAM

There are some who believe national testing of college seniors is a good idea. Koons (2000) thought students, at least those at state institutions in Texas, should be required to take two national achievement tests. One should be in their major field, the other in writing and critical thinking. He pointed to the growing number of nationally normed exams and said that his university, the University of Texas at Austin, should help develop exams for fields where there are none presently available. The results would then be compared to the students' high school grade point average and incoming SAT scores to determine what the student might have reasonably been expected to achieve. Each major is then evaluated by the "value added" through their instruction. Programs in which students do well are rewarded with additional funding. The exams are not "high stakes" for the students in that there are no passing grades, merely a score. They are, obviously, high stakes for the department or program. Koons is pushing such exams for a variety of reasons. Included are the following:

1. It provides employers meaningful information.
2. It levels the playing field for industrious students by allowing them to compare themselves to students from more prestigious institutions.
3. It gives prospective students a means of comparing programs.
4. It will provide a rational basis for funding programs, especially those that are successful.
5. It will identify excellence in teaching and reward those instructors.
6. It will improve the dynamics of teacher–student interaction by making the teacher primarily a tutor or coach rather than an evaluator or gatekeeper. (Koons, 2000, p. 2)

Perhaps the biggest objection to such a test is that professors would end up "teaching to the test." Koons (2000) answered that in the following way:

> It is an error to assume that multiple-choice exams are limited to testing factual knowledge. ETS regularly uses such exams in testing analytical and interpretive skills. In addition, it would be possible to require students to take nationally normed essay tests, such as the GRE Writing Assess-

ment or the ETS Tasks in Critical Thinking exams. Finally, a statewide collaboration between faculty, education consultants and the ETS will make
possible the continuous improvement and refinement of the Subject
Exams and Major Field Tests. For example, it should be possible for the
exams to incorporate essay questions and problems in critical thinking.
We must devise examinations that test for the skills and knowledge that
we believe to be most important. Instead of "teaching the test" [sic], the
faculty will have, over time, the responsibility of helping to create tests that
effectively test whatever it is that they believe they ought to be teaching.
The quality of instruction can only improve as faculty refine and articulate
the objectives of their instruction. (p. 4)

Koons's initial goal is the creation of statewide tests by subject area. He
believes this will help students looking for programs to be able to compare those programs across institutions. He also believes this will help
determine which programs are functioning at the highest level and de-
serve more funding. It is not high stakes for the students, but it obviously
will become very high stakes for the faculty and their programs. There
are several drawbacks to the scenario outlined by Koons. First, he
makes it sound simple. The meetings to determine statewide learning
outcomes and how to test for those are likely to be far more complicated than Koons estimates. There will be power issues involved as
well. Will the outcomes and test resemble the curriculum of Texas at
Austin or Southwest Texas State? In addition, the results of statewide
tests are likely to give legislators a reason to eliminate programs that do
not do well.

Speaking against exit exams, Georgianna (2000) pointed to Massachusetts and the Comprehensive Assessment System. A high-stakes
high school exam, it originally involved teachers and school administrators in the preparation and testing process. Very shortly, however, state
agencies took over and teachers essentially lost control of their curriculum. Although the example is from high school and not higher education, the lesson seems obvious. When state agencies become involved,
the local system (read as local college) eventually loses control.

A national exit exam is very likely to result in everyone teaching the
same curriculum. It almost has to. If a department wants its students to
do well, it will have to teach the curriculum that the test covers,
whether it specifically has a hand in developing the test. There are very
few circumstances that justify the use of an exit exam at all. What is
happening and is justified is the development of scoring rubrics for a variety of purposes. The role of national organizations such as NCA,
AEJMC, and the BEA should be in the role of facilitators, not as creators
of some national test. As was stated earlier, a national test implies an
agreed-on body of knowledge that can be tested across multitudes of

students and situations. It forces those giving the test to teach to it. One of the great gifts of American higher education to the public is its diversity. The diversity of American curricula, particularly in the area of mass communication, leads to creativity unseen elsewhere. Not everyone who takes scriptwriting gets the same information. Thank goodness. Not everyone who takes mass communication gets the same perspective. Again, thank goodness. A national test moves to narrow the horizon, not expand it. It limits creative possibilities.

The national organizations listed earlier can do a great service by allowing their members to share ideas. Among these ideas should be the wide variety of teaching methods and assignments. Along with those assignments should come scoring rubrics. Instead of just giving a student a grade, the professor explains the grade by being able to specifically point to steps the student has not taken to reach the next level. Instead of just saying, "I got a C," the student can now say, "I got a C and in order to get a B, I need to do the following things." Many mass communication departments now teach a class in critical thinking. Facione and Facione (1994) have developed a scoring rubric for Holistic Critical Thinking. Level 4 (highest) is stated as follows:

> Consistently does all or almost all of the following: Accurately interprets evidence, statements, graphics, questions etc. Identifies the salient arguments (reasons and claims) pro and con. Thoughtfully analyzes and evaluates major alternative points of view. Draws warranted, judicious, non-fallacious conclusions. Justifies key results and procedures, explains assumptions and reasons. Fair-mindedly follows where evidence and reasons lead. (p. 1)

Level 1 (lowest) is stated as follows:

> Consistently does all or almost all of the following: Offers biased interpretations of evidence, statements, graphics, questions, information, or the points of view of others. Fails to identify or hastily dismisses strong, relevant counter-arguments. Ignores or superficially evaluates obvious alternative points of view. Argues using fallacious or irrelevant reasons, and unwarranted claims. Does not justify results or procedures, nor explain reasons. Regardless of the evidence or reasons, maintains or defends views based on self-interest or preconceptions. Exhibits close-mindedness or hostility to reason. (p. 1)

This scoring rubric gives both faculty and students real information about how the assignment was graded. The faculty member can justify to students why they received the grades they did. Scoring rubrics can be created for almost any assignment: TV production, persuasive speeches, newscasts, essays, and so on. The BEA has for years published a variety of syllabi for teachers to use. Perhaps it is now time to do the same for scoring rubrics.

## CONCLUSIONS

It should be fairly obvious that this author does not recommend the use of exit exams. One of the reasons for this conclusion is philosophical. Exit exams imply that a number can be placed on learning. It is a very Western approach to problems. Chemicals can be measured and therefore so can people. There is a single truth and it can be found. Given the complexity and number of variables involved in learning, this strikes me as false pride. It also smacks of politics. The second reason is practical. High quality exams take significant time to produce. The process will then have to be repeated yearly. Unless required to do so by the state or your school's administration, utilizing an exit exam is a waste of time, energy, and resources. Any information gathered will not be predictive or generalizable and hence lack usefulness. The creation of a high-quality exam is difficult within the confines of a single course. The creation of an exam that adequately covers an entire major is almost impossible. To create a new exam each year that adequately covers the entire major is impossible. There are significantly better ways to fulfill an accrediting agency's call for direct student assessment. Several are available in other chapters.

## REFERENCES

American Association for Higher Education, American College Personnel Association, National Association of Student Personnel Administrators. (1998, June). *Powerful partnerships: A shared responsibility for learning.* Retrieved December 8, 2003, from http://www.aahe.org/assessment/joint.htm

American Educational Research, American Psychological Association, National Council on Measurement in Education. (1999). *Standards for educational and psychological testing.* Washington, DC: American Educational Research Association.

Barrington, L. (2003). Less assessment, more learning. *Academe, 89,* 29–31.

Campbell, D. T., & Stanley, J. C. (1963). *Experimental and quasi-experimental designs for research.* Chicago, IL: Rand McNally.

Davey, L., & Neil, M. (1991). *The case against a national test. Practical assessment, research, & evaluation 2(10).* Retrieved November 12, 2003, from http://pareonline.net/getun.asp?v=2&n=10

Department of Communication, University of Toledo, Assessment plan (2004a). Unpublished document.

Department of Communication, University of Toledo, Student evaluation scoring rubric (2004b). Unpublished document.

Dietel, R. J., Herman, J. L., & Knuth, R. A. (1991). *What does research say about assessment?* Retrieved November 5, 2003, from http://www.rcrel.org/sdrs/areas/stw_esys/4assess.htm

Facione, P., & Facione, N. (1994). *Holistic critical thinking scoring rubric.* Retrieved January 28, 2003, from http://www.insightassessment.com/pdf_files/rubric.pdf

Frary, R. B. (2002). More multiple-choice item writing do's and don'ts. In L. M. Rudner & W. D. Schafer (Eds.), *What teachers need to know about assessment* (pp. 75–80). Washington, DC: National Education Association.

Georgiana, D. (2000). *Tests would show that politics rule.* Retrieved December 7, 2004, from http://www.aft.org/publications/on_campus/spet00/speakout.html

Haladyna, T. M. (1999). *Developing and validating multiple-choice test items* (2nd ed.). Mahwah, NJ: Lawrence Erlbaum Associates, Inc.

Haley, E., & Jackson, D. (1995). A conceptualization of assessment for mass communication programs. *Journalism Educator, 50*(1), 26–34.

Higher Learning Commission/North Central Association. (2002). *Assessment of student academic achievement: Levels of implementation. In addendum to the handbook of accreditation* (2nd ed.). Chicago: North Central Association of Colleges and Schools.

Joint Commission on Standards for Educational Evaluation. (2003). *The student evaluation standards.* Thousand Oaks, CA: Corwin Press, Inc.

Kehoe, J. (2002). Writing multiple-choice test items. In L. M. Rudner & W. D. Schafer (Eds.), *What teachers need to know about assessment* (pp. 69–74). Washington, DC: National Education Association.

Koons, R. C. (2000, March). The t.e.a.t.h. proposal: Reforming higher education through state-wide examinations. Retrieved January 21, 2004, from http://www.utexas.edu/cola/depts/philosophy/faculty/Koons/TEATHE.html

Mansilla, V. B., & Gardner, H. (1998). What are the qualities of understanding? In M. S. Wiske (Ed.), *Teaching for understanding* (pp. 161–196). San Francisco: Jossey-Bass.

Moore, D. (1992). *Using tests for assessment, assessment workbook.* Muncie, IN: Ball State University.

Moskal, B. M. (2002). Scoring rubrics: What, when and how? In L. M. Rudner & W. D. Schafer (Eds.), *What teachers need to know about assessment* (pp. 86–94). Washington, DC: National Education Association.

Moskal, B. M., & Leydens, J. A. (2002). Scoring rubric development: Validity and reliability. In L. M. Rudner & W. D. Schafer (Eds.), *What teachers need to know about assessment* (pp. 95–106). Washington, DC: National Education Association.

Osterlind, S. J. (1998). *Constructing test items: Multiple-choice, constructed response, performance, and other formats* (2nd ed.). Boston: Kluwer Academic.

Palomba, C. A., & Banta, T. W. (1999). *Assessment essentials: Planning, implementing and improving assessment in higher education.* San Francisco: Jossey-Bass.

Rodriguez, M. C. (2002). Choosing an item format. In G. Tindal & T. M. Haladyna (Eds.), *Large-scale assessment programs for all students* (pp. 213–232). Mahwah, NJ: Lawrence Erlbaum Associates, Inc.

Rylander, C. K. (2000, December). *Examine giving public universities greater flexibility and increasing accountability. In recommendation of the Texas comptroller.* Retrieved November 19, 2003, from *http://www.e-texas.org/recommend/ch06/ed04.html*

Wiske, M. S. (1998). *Teaching for understanding.* San Francisco: Jossey-Bass.

# APPENDIX A

## Student Evaluation Portfolio Rubric

| Core Objective | Nothing | Naïve | Novice | Apprentice | Master |
|---|---|---|---|---|---|
| Presentation: Student will exhibit the ability to appropriately explain or package a concept or message directed to a specified audience and/or situation. | | | | | |
| Theory/Ethics/History: Student will exhibit knowledge and be conversant with general laws, values principles of inherited wisdom and empirical research in the field of communication. | | | | | |
| Information Analysis/Critical Thinking: The student will exhibit knowledge and ability to evaluate sources and processes of information-manufacture in the modern world, including the ability to produce and defend new knowledge according to the conventions and standards demanded by modern, scientific open societies. | | | | | |
| Applied Knowledge: The student will exhibit the ability to apply the range of communication concepts/skills to solve current social/organizational problems. | | | | | |

## Scoring Rubric Definitions

Master:

1. Corresponds to ordinal level of "excellent" in demonstrated knowledge/ability in the core objective.
2. Fluent, in-depth knowledge of theory, practices, techniques, contexts, formats and conventions related to core objective.
3. Thoroughly grounded in disciplinary knowledge related to core objective and can relate knowledge to other disciplines.
4. Can construct/critique knowledge and/or understand processes of knowledge construction.
5. Ability to interpret and act on the world.
6. Can explain or demonstrate knowledge in creative way.

7. Can combine disciplines for performances/demonstrations of knowledge.
8. Excellent, powerful expression, grammar, syntax, composition abilities.

Apprentice:

1. Corresponds to ordinal level of "good" in demonstrated knowledge/ability in the core objective.
2. Good grounding in disciplinary knowledge.
3. Can explore opportunities and consequences of knowledge.
4. Understands knowledge construction is a complex process initiated by others in the field.
5. Good expression, grammar, syntax, composition abilities.
6. Adequate knowledge of theory, practices, techniques, contexts, formats, and conventions related to core objective.

Novice:

1. Corresponds to ordinal level of "fair" in demonstrating knowledge/ability in the core objective.
2. Knowledge limited to rituals of testing and school.
3. "Rehearsed" connection between and among ideas.
4. Understands knowledge only as a step-by-step process.
5. Validity of knowledge depends on external authority.
6. Fair expression, grammar, syntax, composition abilities.
7. Fair, but quite limited knowledge of theory, practices, techniques, contexts, formats and conventions related to core objective.

Naïve:

1. Corresponds to ordinal level of "poor" in demonstrated knowledge/ability in the core objective.
2. Little or no connection between the classroom and the real world.
3. Little or no consideration of the purposes or uses of knowledge.
4. Poor grammar, syntax, expression, composition abilities.
5. Poor knowledge of theory, practices, techniques, contexts, formats and conventions related to core objective.

Nothing:

1. Corresponds to ordinal level of "failing" in demonstrated knowledge/ability in the core objective.
2. Incoherent or irrelevant work, or absence of any apparent meaningful knowledge relating to the core objective.
3. Lack of demonstrated knowledge of theory, practices, techniques, contexts, formats and conventions related to core objective.

This Student Evaluation Scoring Rubric was developed by the Department of Communication of the University of Toledo. It was developed with the aid of Martha Stone Wiske's book titled, *Teaching for Understanding* (1998). The category titles are from Mansilla and Gardner (1998).

# Direct Measures: Embedded "Authentic" Assessment

Stacey O. Irwin
*Department of Communication and Theatre*
*Millersville University*

*Assessment is authentic when we anchor testing in the kind of work real people do, rather than merely eliciting easy-to-score responses to simple questions. Authentic assessment is true assessment of performance because we thereby learn whether students can intelligently use what they have learned in situations that increase approximate adult situations, and whether they can innovate in new situations.*
—Wiggins (1998, p. 21)

Media and Communication curricula focus on work about real people, with real experiences, and real responses. It makes sense then, that a media curriculum assessment plan would only seem valid and ethical if it were authentic and if it were embedded in the curriculum where it surrounded the day-to-day work in the classroom. It seems odd, almost, that there would be another choice. Media educators are often engaged in authentic and embedded assessment without realizing it. Formalizing the relation is finally putting the name with the face of what has been done for years. It is what we do when we teach our craft, when we grade our media projects, and when we evaluate student writing portfolios.

Authentic assessment is not about choosing quantitative or qualitative methodologies for evaluation, but about designing activities and projects in our courses that most appropriately relate the realism of the media discipline for students, allowing them to practice and experience the subject, and then reflecting on the experience to accomplish greater learning and understanding within the curriculum. This chapter explores the roots of authentic and embedded assessment and paves the way for designing a more formal authentic assessment plan within media curricula.

## WHAT DOES IT MEAN?

The etymological roots of the words "authentic" and "embedded" reveal the crux of this kind of assessment plan. An assessment plan is "authentic" when, honoring its etymological roots, it is real, not false or copied, genuine, and verified in its approach. The Greek word stems from *authentikos,* reminding us that authentic means original, primary, at first hand, and is rooted in the notion of doing something oneself. Authentic assessment is rooted in efforts that many communication-minded individuals strive for in their pedagogical approach and so it is a natural fit as an evaluative process.

The etymological roots of the word "embedded" suggest a kind of fixing into a surrounding mass, surrounded tightly or firmly, enveloped or enclosed in an essential way. The media educator becomes embedded in the work and the assessment becomes embedded in the curriculum. Embedded assessment becomes the real work of the teacher because it is embedded in the whole of the course content, and ideally, in the curriculum itself.

Authentic learning is the authentic root of embedded assessment and means "higher-order learning that is used in solving problems that are present in their context" (Glatthorn, 1999, p. 25). Authentic tasks are paramount in understanding and interpreting if and when authentic learning is underway. Developing authentic tasks involves the creation of a clearly defined and shared performance outcome. This is often stated through learning goals and defined through prompts and rubrics. A prompt is a highly descriptive and informative statement about the goals of the assessment task. A rubric is a scoring instrument that categorizes the finished task and places the work in specific levels of competency. The prompt and the rubric are designed to communicate greater correlation between what that student needs to do and what the instructor will be looking for the student to achieve.

Authentic tasks also focus on students' abilities to draw on knowledge learned in prerequisite courses or core classes. This holistic approach solidifies understanding. The authentic assessment task calls the student to think through important themes relevant to the content being taught. And, the task is embedded within an overarching context or real-world application (Oosterhof, 2003). One of the ambiguities in understanding the notion of real-world application is distinguishing the way the task will be completed. "[R]eal-world applications involve direct applications of knowledge that are highly relevant to situations outside the classroom" (Oosterhof, 2003, p. 158) but not necessarily a specific activity that a student might participate in at the work place. An assessment plan that strives for realism in its context through practice and performance will most appropriately achieve the goals of authentic and embedded assessment.

Learning occurs in degrees. To accomplish notions of authentic assessment at different degrees in the learning, a media educator may want to consider a high degree of realism or authenticity in a variety of different kinds of projects in different classes throughout the media major. An identification test might be appropriate when learning a new kind of software or technology or understanding an organizational structure. A performance test might be useful in a broadcast performance course. A portfolio of work samples might achieve authentic learning in a public relations campaigns class. A research project or hands-on experience might work best in a capstone course or senior-level video production course (Gronlund, 1998). A historical understanding of authentic and embedded kinds of assessment will better solidify an understanding of how a media educator might consider a formal move to this kind of assessment plan. Discussion on shaping an authentic assessment plan and examples of four different authentic assessment tasks are illustrated at the end of this chapter.

## THE HISTORICAL CONTEXT

The authentic assessment movement started in the Kindergarten through 12th-grade (K–12) educational tradition, but has moved through the ranks of higher education in recent years. In the last decade of the 20th century, the emphasis moved away from multiple choice standardized forms of assessment testing in the primary and secondary classrooms and toward a more authentic approach to assessment. The notion of authentic assessment is bundled along with direct assessment and performative assessment as a new way of thinking through alternative assessment (Mabry, 1999). Grant Wiggins, often lauded as the father of the authentic assessment movement, paved the way for greater understanding of this new focus. Wiggins (1998) suggested that assessment that allows the context of the experience to show through is the most authentic kind of assessment design: "Assessment ought to be educative in the basic sense that students are entitled to direct testing that educates them about the purpose of schooling and the nature of adult work" (p. 22). Wiggins's work also provides a basic work print for understanding the authenticity of a task.

Higher education has also taken a turn in assessment efforts. Although college pedagogy was often designed around professional goals and theoretical constructs that were applicable to real-world activities, student achievement was often measured through multiple-choice tests, especially to assess outcomes in a course through a final exam. Large-scale and less relevant assessment projects and evaluations have recently moved toward "regular instructional activities . . . that closely reflect everyday campus activities" (Palomba & Banta, 1999, p. xii). This new turn has introduced the higher education curriculum to the kinds of assessment in development in the K–12 classroom. Portfolios and other kinds of formative assessments have become a popular and useful alternative to other less significant forms of evaluation.

Authentic assessments within the higher education curriculum are largely based on performative measures that closely reflect learning goals designed for a course and draw on the natural goals of a specific educational process (Palomba & Banta, 1999). Mabry (1999) suggested that "authenticity is a matter of degree, some tasks and some performances are more authentic or lifelike than others" (p. 44). For example, students in a scriptwriting class would find that a naturally assessable conclusion to their course would be the creation of a specific kind of script. Students in the visual arts would strive to create a visual work based on discipline-specific models or rating sheets from a video or film festival or contest. Persuasion students might be assessed through public debate on a relevant cultural or political topic. Media law students might write letters to the Federal Communications Commission regarding antitrust issues or ownership in the media. Students in a media history course might write a mock feature article for a magazine that cites specific historical movements and international development through the decades with a conclusion for relevance in today's media-driven society. Again, when the tasks are embedded in the curriculum and the coursework of a specific subject area, the assessment becomes a smooth movement among course goals, program goals, and assessment goals.

Suskie (2004) suggested that these kinds of authentic experiences are embedded assessments: "[P]rogram assessments that are embedded into coursework—often require far less work than add-on assessments" (p. 103). The assignments are already part of the course curriculum so the assessment becomes a natural fit when trying to understand the learning taking place in a program or major area of study. Media educators today are most likely already completing their own classroom assessment as part of the everyday process of educating. Authentic program assessment that is embedded in the curriculum becomes a natural extension of the entire assessment process for the university.

## The Performance Movement

Authentic and embedded assessments nest within a larger explanatory assessment notion called performance assessment. This kind of assessment is focused on students' abilities to demonstrate their skills. If students understand what is expected of them, they become part of the assessment process because they can accurately begin to self assess. This comes back to the very core of assessment, the ability to "educate and improve student performance, not merely to audit it" (Wiggins, 1998, p. 7).

Again, this kind of assessment plan works well for media educators because students are largely graded based on their performance in projects, presentations, and writing assignments. These real-life tasks enfold the assessment process and provide one major focus for student learning. Suskie (2004) suggested that for performative assessment to be valid, students need to be prompted or told what is expected of them, and then they need a scoring guide or rubric to complete the evaluative scoring. This merging of learning and assessment provides the right message to the student and faculty and achieves an authentic goal of measuring student learning. Arter and McTighe (2001) plainly stated that performative assessment means "the students have actually done what ever it is that you want them to be able to do, as opposed to an approximation . . . the idea is to keep the assessment as close as possible to the skills, knowledge, and abilities that are of interest" (p. 46).

But how can media educators ensure authentic performance? One group of researchers suggest that construction of knowledge, disciplined inquiry, and values toward lifelong learning shape an authentic assessment plan (Wiggins, 1998). Construction of knowledge suggests that student work emphasizes high order thinking skills and students' abilities to consider the variety of alternatives in the learning process. Disciplined inquiry focuses on core content knowledge within the media discipline and written communication allows students to elaborate on the core content knowledge. Lifelong learning allows students to view the world beyond the classroom experience as it relates to the media field and involves the community and other professionals in the "real world" (Wiggins, 1998).

## A BIT OF VOCABULARY

Each assessment design carries it's own nomenclature or vocabulary and authentic and embedded assessments are no different. Authentic assessment can be either formative or summative in nature. Formative assessment occurs throughout the semester, as students turn in projects, papers, and class work according to the course syllabus. Formative assessments allow the teacher to adjust teaching and learning and provide feedback throughout the learning process (Suskie, 2004). Summative assessments are more of a capstone experience that provide students with a chance to work through a project or idea that will be used in an assessment evaluation that may be reported to an external audience (Suskie, 2004). Both approaches can incorporate authentic assessment and be embedded in the curriculum.

Assessment efforts can also center on direct measures or indirect measures. Again, authentic assessment can work in each of these scenarios. Direct measures involve specific outcomes that point specifically to conclusive learning. Direct measures can involve written work or performance evaluated through a rubric specifically designed for the assessment project, portfolio evaluation, or student reflection based on stated learning goals and outcomes. In contrast, indirect measures offer probable signs that learning is occurring but the evidence is less clear (Suskie, 2004). Internship or co-op experiences, student evaluation forms, and course grades are all examples of indirect learning.

One additional key understanding to lay the groundwork for the creation of a successful authentic assessment process involves understanding the difference between objective and subjective assessment. Objective assessment is a "paint by numbers" approach that illustrates a breadth of knowledge that does not need expert evaluators. It involves objective tests with one clear answer that can be interpreted through an answer key. Authentic assessment is clearly situated in the subjective category of assessment. This kind of assessment focuses on skills not well defined through objective testing, promotes deep and lasting learning, and demonstration of a large number of learning goals (Suskie, 2004). Discipline-specific experts are needed to evaluate subjective assessments because there are nuances in the evaluative process that prevent a less meaningful generic evaluation. Appropriate and thoughtful summative assessment, like authentic assessment, can provide the kind of reportable evidence mandated by the higher education boards of many states. Although more time consuming, summative authentic assessments that are performative and embedded can illustrate to your institution that lasting learning is being achieved consistently over time.

## A SHARED RESPONSIBILITY

An assessment plan designed with authenticity in mind needs to be evaluated in an authentic way by all of the players involved in the learning. Students, community leaders, teachers, and others must all come together to design a plan that meets assessment goals. Students are the most often overlooked stakeholders in this process. True authentic assessment brings students into the evaluation process in many ways. Attaching the assessment rubric to the syllabus at the beginning of the semester is one way to begin achieving this goal. Students quickly gain an understanding of the aim of their tasks and projects when the evaluation is part of the initial understanding of the course. Students who are part of the evaluative process are active learners because they think "about what counts as quality and developing personal standards of quality" (Mabry, 1999, p. 71). Inviting students to be part of the initial brainstorming about their assessment plan also allows them to play a part in the process that they will be involved in for many years. It raises the level of understanding about an assessment process early in learning and increases respect for an often-mandated process that may have far-reaching implications for their education.

Community leaders, outside reviewers, and internship coordinators who are active in the media field may provide additional support and understanding by participating in the assessment process. Campus members and administrators are also part of this process because some assessment results are reported to off-campus sources. The Middle States Commission on Higher Education, in their guide *Student Learning Assessment: Options and Resources* (2003), clearly stressed the variety of players in the assessment process and the role each needs to play in the development of an assessment program.

Most important, the teacher actively engaged in authentic assessment becomes a dynamic participant in the classroom experience. Teachers find that through authentic assessment, their understanding of learning in general and the particular learning their students are engaged in is illustrated in a more concrete way, and in a variety of ways, and allows for more depth in the feedback and evaluation process. Many students ask, "How am I doing? Authentic assessment allows the instructor to answer in a variety of different ways based on the authentic tasks the student has completed (Darling-Hammond, Ancess, & Falk, 1995). The increased depth in this conversation gives the student a more grounded direction to go toward to attain what he or she needs to be successful in his or her chosen media field. An instructor who is engaged in authentic assessment stresses the objectives "explain; organize; interpret; evaluate; synthesize" as the assessment task or classroom activity unfolds (Glatthorn, 1999, p. 30). This move toward metacognition through questioning the learning process as it unfolds helps students both deconstruct the problem and build toward understanding. A teacher that provides appropriate structure throughout the learning process and supports a positive learning environment by welcoming feedback in the assessment process most fully achieves the goals of a positive authentic assessment experience.

Timely reflection and feedback to the student are two important steps in the shared teacher–student experience of authentic assessment. An embedded assessment approach may be so well interfaced into a curriculum that students are unaware that assessment is in process. Glatthorn (1999) suggested the following features of feedback:

> The feedback is timely, delivered as soon as possible after the performance.
>
> The feedback is primarily objective, based upon clear criteria and specific evidence.
>
> The feedback is multiple, using several sources.
>
> The feedback is constructive, emphasizing both the strengths demonstrated and some of a learner's responsibilities to support the learning, reflect on the aspects that can be improved. (pp. 37–38)

Students who understand that learning, cooperation, and performance are being assessed are better able to articulate through writing, the way they work through the process and the learning (Glatthorn, 1999). Oftentimes students feel that their job is to sit in a room while the instructor rolls out a Power Point presentation from which they can take notes. The notion of active learning that is addressed early on in the classroom provides a context for authentic assessment efforts. Students need to understand that the instructor will expect active learning. Sometimes this facilitation and articulation may come in the form of reflective essays and other times this can be accomplished through learning contracts or action plans.

Because authentic assessment may take the form a group project, it is important to assign each learner a specific piece of the process to make learning possible for all students. A learner's ability to individually think through the learning process is important to authentic assessment because authentic learning is best served on the individual level. This individual accountability toward learning fosters a student's ability to acquire new knowledge and use it to understand the subject area or discipline (Glatthorn, 1999).

## CONFIRMING AUTHENTICITY

The process of creating an authentic assessment begins with finding the appropriate ways to embed the assignments and projects within the curriculum. Some media programs might choose to start from a strategic plan to work this through, whereas others might find an assessment committee or curriculum committee the most appropriate place to discuss and discover ways to embed assessable performance tasks and activities to integrate authentic assessment into the curriculum. Still others might start from the classroom and build out from there. Angelo and Cross (1993) used a notion they call "Teaching Goals Inventory" or TGI, to begin assessment at the classroom level (p. 8).

Linking a strategic plan with an assessment plan provides a vision to guide learning goals and learning outcomes for a program (Baron & Boschee, 1995). This emphasis allows authentic assessment to gain the value it deserves in the educational process while it begins to take on more of a central curricular role and less of an emphasis as additional service-based "busy work." The instructor's role is shifted to teacher-scholar, as the assessment becomes research about teaching. Many colleges and universities have designed a strategic plan. Adapting such a plan into a media department program is a positive way to bring a departmental vision and learning emphasis in line and provides an enriching opportunity for faculty to talk through the learning goals they aim for their students to achieve.

Thinking through how the curriculum and the assessment approach link together is an important discussion. Scott (2001) noted the following: "there is no single method for formative assessment, but rather a need for varying the styles of both pedagogy and formative assessment to match the different components of a curriculum according to the differing nature of the aims that these components serve" (p. 21). Some experts note that aligning assessment goals with curriculum and instruction is the best way to ensure that the time spent on assessment is spent wisely. "[A]ssessment should provide a clear understanding of how we—as teachers and students—are doing on attaining these goals. Everything from instruction to "curriculum and assessment reaches toward the same goals" (Blum & Arter, 1996, p. IV–1:1). Workshops, faculty retreats, and grants are also an important resource to tap into while thinking through these kinds of authentic assessment issues. They are important resources in the collaborative efforts of formative authentic assessment.

Each assignment within the media curriculum must correspond, in some way, to the variety of ways media is part of the fabric of today's society. The bottom line is providing students with authentic tasks that provide provable results while training students to be effective communicators and media makers. "Using authentic tasks provide validity, in that they tell us about students' performance on important aspects of the domain that are generally neglected in multiple-choice and short answer tests . . ." (Scott, 2001, p. 166). Options for fashioning an authentic assessment include but are not limited to essays, journal writing, performances and projects, identification tests, posters, reaction papers, labs, reports, and a variety of writing samples. Essays and journal writing also differ from summative kinds of short-answer tests because they allow students to develop and work through ideas around an overarching principle or notion that is central to understanding one's discipline.

## SOME ADDITIONAL CONSIDERATIONS

Oftentimes embarking on a new direction for assessment can cause concerns within the entire idea of assessment. Authentic assessment is often considered a time-consuming process or a process that creates difficulty in gaining reliable assessment results. Authentic assessment must rely on valid, concise, and clear rubrics and scoring sheets. This is also considered a time-consuming undertaking. Individuals involved in authentic assessment spend a great deal of time in the beginning of the process, working through rubrics with colleagues and others in their field of study. Fortunately, rubric designs are often available through a variety of print and online sources. Additionally, many instructors have designed parts of rubrics for their own grading in a specific course. Coming together for an initial brainstorming session can be a beginning step in creating valid instruments for assessment.

Another common early concern is ensuring that performance assessment tasks are actually authentic in nature. "All authentic assessments are performance assessments, but the inverse is not true" (Oosterhof, 2003, p. 147). A real-world application "does not necessarily refer to activities in which students will directly participate later in life. Instead, real-world applications involve direct applications of knowledge that are highly relevant to situations outside the classroom" (Oosterhof, 2003, p. 158). This focus on the knowledge itself can direct the creation of authentic tasks. Also, the tasks that involve student "constructed responses" (Mabry, 1999, p. 17) instead of making a selection from a list of possibilities move toward authentic assessment.

It is also important that the players involved in assessment evaluation and scoring understand the rubric and the curriculum or discipline under evaluation. Assessment training for evaluators and meetings designed to discuss the rubric right before the assessment begins are helpful ways of educating individuals to increase validity and reliability in the evaluation process. Because authentic assessment is often not easily correlated through comparisons of student work from other places, encouraging and fostering students to enter media festivals, script contests, and other regional or national evaluative events or aligning program rubrics to these kinds of evaluative ratings helps solidify a comparative nature to authentic assessment efforts.

## SHAPING YOUR AUTHENTIC ASSESSMENT PLAN

The next step after choosing to move forward with an authentic assessment plan is to design the tasks and create a prompt and rubric for each assignment. Again, a prompt is the clear articulation of the assignment and the rubric is the scoring guide that will determine the assessable results.

The following section describes ideas for different kinds of authentic assessment projects for media classes, along with sample prompts and rubrics. Each idea can easily be expanded, pared down, or altered to describe a different task. The real focus is on the clear articulation of the authentic assessment task and the effective grading or assessment of each task so that the work being completed for the class and for the assessment reveals learning in concrete ways. Walvoord and Anderson (1998) suggested that grading needs to be the "process by which a teacher assesses student learning through classroom tests and assignments, the context in which good teachers establish that process, and the dialogue that surrounds grades and defines their meaning to various audiences" (p. 1). These three guiding principles need to be at the heart of authentic assessment evaluation embedded in a curriculum. Breaking down each of these notions provides a direction for beginning an authentic assessment plan.

Clear communication between a student and an instructor begins with a clear and well-written prompt. Students begin their authentic task with a clear vision of the work to be done when a prompt clearly illustrates the expectations of the assignment. Although an instructor's verbal instructions and syllabus often spells out course objectives, a list of assignments, and the weight of assignments along with goals and teaching philosophy, when students begin work on an assignment, they generally focus only on the information provided for a specific graded assignment. The requirements of the prompt need to reflect the learning goals as closely as possible and what the prompt actually requires students to do in the assignment. A prompt cannot be too vague or too detailed. Students need to negotiate the problem solving in a way that keeps the task authentic (Smith, Smith, & De Lisi, 2001). A restricted-response prompt can be designed to invoke a fairly narrow and similar response from each student and an extended-response prompt gives students an opportunity to move through an issue in a variety of ways (Suskie, 2004, p. 1). In either case, a prompt is designed to clearly articulate the assignment so students know the direction to go and student learning can be evaluated.

Students who receive a clearly defined and well-written prompt also need to understand the specific criteria that will be used in the evaluation process. This is called a rubric, scoring guide, or grading criteria (Suskie, 2004, p. 1). Arter and McTighe (2001) suggested that a rubric needs to be designed based on the kinds of tasks in which students will be involved. Will the rubric be generic or specific? How can an instructor ensure that it is effective in measuring learning? Most instructors have an informal rating sheet or checklist on paper or in memory. A rubric formalizes the process and spans the wide variety of options in the grading process. A rubric also allows the student to understand the thought process behind the instructor's letter grade decision. A rubric alleviates notions that the student did not understand the instructor's expectations or that the instructor did or didn't "like" the work, as if it were an arbitrary and personal artistic or aesthetic judgment.

To design a rubric, begin by loosely listing the criteria known to be important in the authentic task. Then, fine tune the list and move it into a scoring format that makes sense for anyone that might be involved in evaluation like external experts or other instructors. Also, use other kinds of scoring guides like professional models of competence or rubrics from other courses or disciplines as examples of ways to get started on a design (Arter & McTighe, 2001). This formal move toward grading articulation heightens the effectiveness of the evaluation and provides important expectations and feedback in the process. A rubric is most often designed like a checklist, rating scale, descriptive or holistic rating scale. These kinds of formats provide an instructor with the ability to clearly think through specific learning goals for the assignment, create a meaningful problem that corresponds to the goals, make the assignment worthwhile to the learning environment, and create clear and specific instructions pointed toward the desired outcome (Suskie, 2004).

The most effective rubrics articulate the key learning goals of the assignment, the characteristics that denote a "most correctly complete" assignment, and a list of all elements that are to be included in the assignment. Clearly articulating the completed goals an institution is looking for when grading the assignment gives students a good target to shoot for as they try to accomplish the assignment (Suskie, 2004). In most cases, the student can be given the rubric when the prompt and assignment are given so they fully understand the nature of the final evaluation.

For example, an instructor might want to use an identification test to serve as an authentic experience in a lower level production class, scriptwriting workshop, public relations campaign class, or media management course. This kind of task can be seen as authentic when the experience allows students to work through some definable goal that is demonstrated in a media career. Building a demonstration, work plan, program proposal, lighting grid, staging grid, flowchart, graph, chart, or an equipment diagnostic would be similar in nature to the notion of an identification test exercise.

The prompt would clearly state the goals of the identification test and the expected outcome from the work. What do you expect students to achieve at the completion of this identification test? What level of detail needs to be articulated by the student? How should the student work be formatted? Including page length specifications and suggestions on how a student might most effectively use his or her time in completing the test in or out of class time are helpful to the final learning goals and build an authentic nature to the assignment. It is also helpful for students to know if the instructor is willing to look at drafts of the work. The rubric would clearly state the goals in an evaluative scoring sheet that lists each area of competence, a list of written elements that need to be included in the task, and an evaluation using a sliding scale or scoring instrument that clearly states the level of competency achieved on the identification test (for four samples of authentic assessment tasks, see Appendixes A, B, C, and D.)

## FINAL THOUGHTS ABOUT EMBEDDED, AUTHENTIC ASSESSMENT

"Authenticity is a matter of degree, some tasks and some performances are more authentic or lifelike than others. Some cognitively useful activities better lend themselves to real or realistic demonstration of skill than others" (Mabry, 1999, p. 44).

Authenticity and assessment are both about a desire to know if students are really learning the knowledge and skills that they need to learn, to be prepared for the next step in their education and career. A variety of activities are beneficial in the creation of an educated person. An assessment plan created by a group of informed and interested instructors who are thoughtful in the curricular process and committed to the need to evaluate student learning will automatically move toward an authentically designed assessment plan. And it is indeed a movement. Sometimes the process is slow, starting with one instructor and one classroom experience. Sometimes authentic assessment can move in large sweeping strokes because the notion of authenticity is captured by an entire program or university. Either way, the strategies and examples given here can either influence a movement to start, continue, or change direction on a unique trail toward something embedded in the curriculum, and within the assessment process, that is real, genuine, and verified in its approach.

## REFERENCES

Angelo, T., & Cross, P. (1993). *Classroom assessment techniques: A handbook for college teachers* (2nd ed.). San Francisco: Jossey-Bass.

Arter, J., & McTighe, J. (2001). *Scoring rubrics in the classroom: Using performance criteria for assessing and improving student performance.* Thousand Oaks, CA: Corwin Press, Inc.

Baron, M., & Boschee, F. (1995). *Authentic assessment: The key to unlocking student success.* Lancaster, PA: Technomic Publishing Company, Inc.

Blum, R., & Arter, J. (1996). *A handbook for student performance assessment in an era of restructuring.* Alexandria, VA: Association for Supervision and Curriculum Development.

Darling-Hammond, L., Ancess, J., & Falk, B. (1995). *Authentic assessment in action: Studies of schools and students at work.* New York: Teachers College Press.

Glatthorn, A. (1999). *Performance standards & authentic learning.* Larchmont, NY: Eye On Education Inc.

Gronlund, N. (1998). *Assessment of student achievement* (6th ed.). Boston: Allyn & Bacon.

Mabry, L. (1999). *Portfolios plus: A critical guide to alternative assessment.* Thousand Oaks, CA: Corwin Press, Inc.

Middle States Commission on Higher Education. (2003). *Student learning assessment: Options and resources.* Philadelphia: Middle States Commission on Higher Education.

Oosterhof, A. (2003). *Developing and using classroom assessments* (3rd ed.). Upper Saddle River, NJ: Pearson Education.

Palomba, C., & Banta, T. (1999). *Assessment essentials: Planning, implementing, and improving assessment in higher education.* San Francisco: Jossey-Bass.

Scott, D. (2001). *Curriculum and assessment.* London: Ablex.

Smith, J., Smith, L., & De Lisi, R. (2001). *Natural classroom assessment: Designing seamless instruction and assessment.* Thousand Oaks, CA: Corwin Press, Inc.

Suskie, L. (2004). *Assessment of student learning: A common sense guide.* Bolton, MA: Anker Publishing.

Walvoord, B., & Anderson, V. (1998). *Effective grading; a tool for learning and assessment.* San Francisco: Wiley.

Wiggins, G. (1998). *Educative assessment: Designing assessments to inform and improve student performance.* San Francisco: Jossey-Bass.

## APPENDIX A

### Media and Politics

Authentic Task: During class time next week, you will be asked to create an administrative flowchart of the elected and paid politicians in the city you plan to live in after graduation.

Prompt: This assignment is designed to build and test your knowledge about the political system in the city you expect to move to once you graduate. As a member of the media community, it is vitally important that you know when you are meeting someone who holds a political office in your community. Understanding the political structure in any community where you will be required to negotiate the political landscape is a highly important and useful skill. This understanding is specifically geared to any media business, including television or radio reporting, campaigning, developing advertising strategies, or media research, that involves interfacing with the political community. You need to come to class with all of the knowledge you need to create a flowchart of key political positions. This means you need to do your research this week. The instructor will provide you with the list of positions during class time that need to be included on the flowchart. A student may use his or her own personal notes during the class time for the creation of the political flowchart. Each student must complete individual work.

The completed assignment should clearly list, in flowchart form, all of the stated political offices in hierarchical order beginning with the most important position at the top. The positions need to be color-coded based on their status: elected or appointed. The flowchart must be completed during one class period. This assignment should take 4–6 hours of pre-class research. Large pieces of paper will be provided in class for the creation of your flowcharts.

Rubric: The flowchart rubric clearly states the goals that the instructor will evaluate. Figure 1 illustrates a rating scale rubric for a flowchart identification test in a Media and Politics course.

## Media and Politics Political Structure Flow Chart: An Identification Test Rating Scale Rubric

|  | Excellent | Competent | Incomplete |
|---|---|---|---|
| The flowchart is well-organized in a hierarchical pattern with the highest position at the top. | ☐ | ☐ | ☐ |
| The flowchart is neatly printed. | ☐ | ☐ | ☐ |
| The flowchart is complete. | ☐ | ☐ | ☐ |
| All names are spelled properly. | ☐ | ☐ | ☐ |
| The information is accurate. | ☐ | ☐ | ☐ |
| Paid and elected officials are appropriately color-coded. | ☐ | ☐ | ☐ |
| Accomplished the stated objectives. | ☐ | ☐ | ☐ |

## APPENDIX B

### Advanced Television Production

Authentic Task: Produce, shoot and edit a five-minute public affairs special interest field segment on a significant issue to young people in this State.

Prompt: This assignment is designed to build on all of your knowledge about television producing and your skills in video production to create a piece of programming that will be appropriate to roll into a local PBS special about issues in this State. You must research a topic, interview three individuals who are players or stakeholders in the discussion, and shoot appropriate b-roll, cut ins, cut-aways and natural sound to accompany the story in the appropriate time allotted. Think audio, think video, think writing, and think presentation! The target demographic: young adults who live in this region.

This segment will not have a reporter or talent within the story but you may use a voice-over as needed. This assignment should take 10 hours of pre-production, 6 hours of production time, and 2–3 hours of post-production. Use the Ariel font for all lower-third titles, with appropriate consideration to readability and graphic presentation.

Rubric: The descriptive and specific rubric clearly states the technical and aesthetic learning goals the instructor will evaluate. Figure 2 illustrates a rating scale rubric for a field segment in an advanced television production course.

## Advanced Television Production Field Segment Combination Rating Scale/Rubric

Please check the appropriate box for each question.

**Sense of Project Grade  A   B   C   D   F**

5- Demonstrates excellent skill, 4- above average skill, 3-average skill, 2-below average skill, 1-poor demonstration of skill, N/A- not able to evaluate this section.

| # | | 5 | 4 | 3 | 2 | 1 | N/A |
|---|---|---|---|---|---|---|---|
| 1 | The quality, angle, color and intensity of light is appropriate for the time of day, apparent source of light within the set/location, character and mood of the segment. | | | | | | |
| 2 | Titles show color compatibility and demonstrate readability, tonal separation, brightness range and safe title limitations and do not interfere with visual content. | | | | | | |
| 3 | Titles and credits remain on screen long enough to be read. | | | | | | |
| 4 | Framing in the shots demonstrates an understanding of the rules of composition. | | | | | | |
| 5 | Cameras are at proper height in relation to the interview subjects and desired psychological effect. | | | | | | |
| 6 | Dollying, trucking, panning, tracking and zooming are smooth and motivated and appropriate to the pace of the production. | | | | | | |
| 7 | All audio is clear and distinct. | | | | | | |
| 8 | Audio levels are appropriately mixed between ambient sound and main sound and are integrated and mixed well from shot to shot. | | | | | | |
| 9 | A variety of sound is used appropriately as part of the storytelling: natural sound, sound bites, music, v/o. | | | | | | |
| 10 | All cuts and transitions are motivated and in harmony with the pace and nature of the story. | | | | | | |
| 11 | Consistent visual perspectives are maintained so as not to confuse the audience. | | | | | | |
| 12 | Except for dramatic effect, the shot selection follows what the audience expects, wants, or needs to see at any given moment. | | | | | | |
| 13 | Shot sequencing is used to build connections throughout the story to build a logical visual statement. | | | | | | |
| 14 | Avoidance of continuity jumps and general continuity errors like jump cuts. | | | | | | |
| 15 | Fluidity and smoothness of editing decisions. | | | | | | |
| 16 | Complexity of shots | | | | | | |
| 17 | Overall effectiveness of storytelling | | | | | | |
| 18 | Overall effectiveness of written, visual and audio continuity.  Does the piece hang together well as a whole. | | | | | | |
| 19 | Overall creativity | | | | | | |
| 20 | Overall effectively produced. | | | | | | |

Overall total___/100                    Row totals_____

This rubric was designed by Stacey Irwin, William Horne, and John MacKerron and is used for assessment purposes in the Department of Electronic Media and Film, Towson University, Towson, MD.

## APPENDIX C

### History of Electronic Media or History of Film

Authentic Task: Research and write a film or electronic media history related article for your local newspaper's special feature section titled: *Does History Repeat Itself?* This task exhibits your ability to explore and synthesize important historical elements of a specific time period within film or electronic media history that you choose and was studied in the class this semester, and introduce the subject in a new or unique way for the average newspaper reader in your community.

Prompt: This assignment is designed to build on all of your knowledge plus additional research, about a specific historical topic in your area of study this semester in a way that might enlighten others who know nothing about your topic and its importance in history. The emphasis is on content and writing abilities. Research and write a paper that explores and synthesizes historical elements of a specific time period studied to a novice audience. Please provide a strong and compelling introduction, body of the paper, and conclusion to your work in an interesting way.

Clearly organize your feature article so it makes sense to the reader and proves your points based on researchable and cited evidence. Write in a way that shows your careful critical thinking on a historical subject based on examples used throughout the semester. Use appropriate grammar, spelling, and documentation in a history-writing style to show your understanding of this kind of writing. Emphasize originality in thought on your chosen topic and try to explore it as deeply as possible in 10–12 pages. This feature article will take approximately 10–15 hours of research with 10–12 sources cited, and the time to thoughtfully write your newspaper article.

Rubric: The scoring rubric clearly states the goals that the instructor will evaluate. Figure 3 illustrates a general history-writing rubric that is designed for use in multiple course sections across a media curriculum. The writing instructors wanted to clearly state each of the levels of evaluation and they also discussed what each category meant before the blind and randomly sampled papers were read. This sample shows a rubric for each level of competence and then an additional scoring sheet.

|  | Needs work | Competent | Well done |
|---|---|---|---|
| **Organization—including Introduction, Body of Paper, Conclusion (20 pts)** | Random organization | Evidence of proficiency in logical organization | Evidence of clear organization, strong intro, body, conclusion. |
| **Content —Research —Documentation (20)** | Limited content development, Limited understanding of research, documentation for content. Few references or indication of research | Fairly deep development, use of research and documentation is clearly proficient | Deep and complex content understanding, use of research and documentation clear and well used. |
| **Critical Thinking Originality (20)** | Limited awareness of critical thinking, cohesion, minimal development, originality | Focused critical thinking and originality | Careful critical thinking, connecting, and originality that indicates substantial understanding. |
| **Mechanics— Grammar, spelling, documentation, (20)** | Many errors in grammar, spelling, documentation Passive jargon Verb tense issues Use of "there" etc. . . . | Few errors in grammar, spelling, documentation | Zero or 1 error in grammar, spelling, documentation |
| **Appropriate response to assignment (10)** | Limited response | Clear and logical response | Precise and rich response. |
| **Appropriateness of style (10)** | Errors in appropriateness | Fairly appropriate of style | Clearly appropriate in style |

Using the history-writing rubric, please rate each anonymous paper

**Name of paper** _____

**Reviewer:** _____

**GRADE you would give this paper (circle)**      A    A-    B+    B    B-    C+    C    C-    D    F

|  | Needs work 10-14 | Competent 15-17 | Well done 18-20 |
|---|---|---|---|
| Organization—including Introduction, Body of Paper, Conclusion (20 pts) |  |  |  |
| Content<br>---Research<br>---Documentation (20) |  |  |  |
| Critical Thinking<br>Originality (20) |  |  |  |
| Mechanics---Grammar, spelling, documentation, (20) |  |  |  |
| Appropriate response to assignment (10) |  |  |  |
| Appropriateness of style (10) |  |  |  |

This rubric was designed by Stacey Irwin, Peter Lev, and Daniel Mydlack and is used for assessment in the Department of Electronic Media and Film, Towson University, Towson, MD.

## APPENDIX D

### Filmmaking

Authentic Task: Create a narrative film that recognizes excellent skill in camera work, audio, sound, lighting, editing and overall effect of film work.

Prompt: This assignment is designed to build on your prior experience in narrative filmmaking as well as to advance you to the next level of understanding in film production. The emphasis is on excellence in camera work, audio, sound, lighting, editing and overall effect of film work. Though estimation of production times may vary greatly, this four to six minute narrative film production project will encompass at least 20–40 hours of preproduction time, 2–3 shoot dates, and 15–20 hours of postproduction editing and audio sweetening work.

Rubric: The scoring rubric clearly states the goals that the instructor and program will evaluate. The scoring categories move from excellent skill to poor skill level. Figure 4 illustrates a rubric that reflects the authentic task of creating a short narrative film. The film instructors wanted to clearly state each of the levels of evaluation. They also discussed what each category meant before the blind and randomly sampled films were viewed. This rubric was designed to span the experience from narrative filmmaker to advanced narrative filmmaker. The same rubric will be used with each successive course (Film I to Film III) to guide the skills student filmmakers will develop in the program. Prerequisite coursework was also considered when creating this rubric so that total learning within the film emphasis of the program major could be assessed. This sample shows a rubric that articulates each level of skill to instructors involved in assessment as well as possible outside reviewers engaging in the film assessment plan. The scoring sheet follows for a more exact scoring.

## Narrative Film Production Rubric

This rubric is focused on five different areas: camera work, audio, sound, lighting, editing and overall effect of film work. Instructors have identified three general areas of assessment for the rubric. Each category reflects curricular values that the instructors in the program want to emphasize with student filmmakers.

| Rubric | Excellent skill | Average skill | Poor Skill |
|---|---|---|---|
| Correct exposure | Correct exposure | Mostly correct exposure with some possible issues | Incorrect exposure |
| Image in focus | Completely in focus | In focus throughout film with one or two problem areas. | Problems with focus throughout film |
| Dynamic frame composition, camera angle, camera subject distance, camera movement if appropriate. | All appropriate to narrative structure and understanding of film. | Mostly appropriate to narrative structure and understanding of film. | Problems understanding narrative structure and understanding the film |
| Coverage is adequate | Excellent coverage | Average coverage | Clear issues in coverage |
| Audio mixed appropriately | Mix that is appropriate to to the film | Generally good mix | Consistent problems with sound mix |
| Good audio levels | Appropriate audio levels throughout film. | Mostly appropriate audio levels throughout film. | Consistent audio level problems throughout piece. |
| Good audio quality | Appropriate audio quality throughout film. | Mostly appropriate audio quality throughout film. | Consistent audio quality problems throughout piece. |
| Appropriate use of ambient sound | Appropriate use of ambient sound throughout film. | Mostly appropriate use of ambient sound throughout film. | Consistent problems with or lack of appropriate ambient sound throughout film. |
| Use of appropriate sound effects, music, and music composition if original | Excellent use of appropriate sound effects, music, and music composition if original | Some use of appropriate sound effects, music, and music composition if original | No use of appropriate sound effects, music, and music composition if original |
| Consistency of light and exposure | Excellent consistency of light and exposure | Some isolated problems with light and exposure | Inconsistent and problematic consistency of light and exposure |
| Appropriate lighting | Excellent lighting that contributes to the entire film | Generally appropriate lighting throughout the film | Inappropriate and problematic lighting |
| Seamless invisibility | Excellent use of seamless invisibility throughout narrative structure | Generally good use of seamless invisibility throughout narrative structure | Lack of understanding of this concept |

| Optimum vantage point. | Audience given information they need at appropriate time | Audience generally given information they need at appropriate time | Audience not given information they need at appropriate time |
|---|---|---|---|
| Consistent visual perspectives are maintained so as not to confuse the audience | Visual perspective maintained | Consistency maintained | Audience confused |
| Develops audience identification with character through POV, close ups, shot-reverse shot patterns | Strong audience identification | Isolated problems with visual perspective | Undeveloped and unclear audience identification |
| Appropriate creative, and originality in use of titles, credits | Original and creative use | Some creativity and appropriate use of titles | Lack of originality and appropriate use of titles |
| Production values: cohesiveness of sets, props, location, costuming | Strong production values | Generally good production values with few isolated problems. | Problematic production values |
| Directing and casting/acting | Good choices in directing, casting and acting | Some good choices in directing, casting and acting | Problematic Directing, casting/acting |
| Create a believable fictional world | Well created believable and fictional world | Mostly believable fictional world. | Does not create a believable fictional world |
| Clearly and effectively forwards the narrative | Excellent in this area | Somewhat forwards narrative | Narrative story is not forwarded |

**Rating Sheet**

The rating sheet is based on the narrative film rubric, but breaks the assessment into five different scoring categories that range from excellent skill to poor demonstration of skill. This allows the evaluation to create a percentage that begins with 100% in the way that a course grade would begin at 100%.

5- demonstrates excellent skill, 4- above average skill, 3-average skill, 2-below average skill,
1-poor demonstration of skill

| # | | 5 | 4 | 3 | 2 | 1 |
|---|---|---|---|---|---|---|
| 1 | Correct exposure | | | | | |
| 2 | Image in focus | | | | | |
| 3 | Dynamic frame composition, camera angle, camera subject distance, camera movement if appropriate. | | | | | |
| 4 | Coverage is adequate | | | | | |
| 5 | Audio mixed appropriately | | | | | |
| 6 | Good audio levels | | | | | |
| 7 | Good audio quality | | | | | |
| 8 | Appropriate use of ambient sound | | | | | |
| 9 | Use of appropriate sound effects, music, and music composition if original | | | | | |
| 10 | Consistency of light and exposure | | | | | |
| 11 | Appropriate lighting | | | | | |
| 12 | Seamless invisibility | | | | | |
| 13 | Optimum vantage point. Audience given information they need at appropriate time | | | | | |
| 14 | Consistent visual perspectives are maintained so as not to confuse the audience | | | | | |

| 15 | Develops audience identification with character through POV, close ups, shot-reverse shot patterns | | | | | |
|----|---|---|---|---|---|---|
| 16 | Appropriate creative, and originality in use of titles, credits | | | | | |
| 17 | Production values: cohesiveness of sets, props, location, costuming | | | | | |
| 18 | Directing and casting/acting | | | | | |
| 19 | Create a believable fictional world | | | | | |
| 20 | Clearly and effectively forwards the narrative | | | | | |

Overall total___/100                          Row totals_____

Overall this project warrants a grade of. . . .   A      B     C     D      F
Semester projects are collected:_____
Semester assessment is conducted:_____

This rating sheet and rubric were designed by Tom Brandau, Greg Faller, Stacey Irwin and Paula Mozen. The rating sheet is used for assessment purposes in the Department of Electronic Media and Film, Towson University, Towson, MD.

# Direct Measures: Portfolios

Ralph Donald
*Department of Mass Communications*
*Southern Illinois University–Edwardsville*

This chapter provides insight into an increasingly popular way to find out, as Jeremy Cohen put it, "What our curriculum and pedagogy is accomplishing," and "What we can do as professional educators to increase student success" (2004). A dozen years ago it was difficult to identify a media education program that required a student to complete a portfolio that summarized his or her undergraduate work. However, at this writing, a single Yahoo search for "portfolio + mass communication" yielded 60 undergraduate programs that required portfolios for this purpose. (This Yahoo search also discovered a number of graduate and certificate programs that required portfolios as part of the application process. Also, Lebanon Valley College's English Department, in which Media Studies is housed, requires a satisfactory student portfolio as a prerequisite to enrolling in their internship course. As well, this survey also discovered colleges and universities that required portfolio projects (scrapbooks, student reviews, and reflections on their media use) as early on as their Introduction to Mass Media courses.

## DEFINING THE PORTFOLIO

What is a portfolio? In addition to the field of education, this term is used by photographers, graphic and fine artists, businesses (to display their work for marketing purposes), and of course, by traders in the stock market. In the academy, many kinds of compilations of student and faculty work are referred to as portfolios. As part of the tenure process, faculty teaching portfolios are common. Student portfolio use and description depend on certain factors, including the educational level (they are in use as early as elementary school) and the discipline (e.g., it's heavily used in English and in other subjects in which students compile a considerable amount of written material). Vavrus called the portfolio "a systematic and organized collection of evidence used by the teacher to monitor growth of the student's knowledge, skills and attitudes" (1990, p. 48). As well, Larson said that the name portfolio "should designate, at least, an ordered compilation of writing [or, in the case of a media student, other media products] ... A portfolio ideally should be a deliberate compilation, gathered according to some plan, for use by an identified reader or readers for specific needs or purposes" (1991, p. 138).

## MEDIA STUDIES PORTFOLIOS

Educators employ portfolios according to their assessment objectives. Even within the disciplines of media studies, the portfolio concept varies. To further this discussion, and to begin to explain the kind of portfolio that a media student might compile at the end of his or her degree program, I offer my own syllabus definition: "The senior portfolio is a compilation of the best coursework and projects you have produced while in college. A portfolio can also include media products you've produced at other colleges before you transferred to this university, work you've produced during your internship or in recent professional media jobs."

## MORE VARIATION IN MEDIA PORTFOLIOS

Although the earlier-mentioned Yahoo survey indicated that most schools use portfolios as a finishing experience, there is no single, nationwide definition of what a media student's portfolio should include or exclude. And this disparity is proper, because portfolios, to be of value as a direct assessment tool, must assess a set of educational outcomes that are unique to an institution and the academic unit.

There are also many different approaches to the evaluation of portfolios. This stems from the fact that evaluation methods must vary according to the unit's prescribed portfolio content. For example, this content might be confined to a student's work produced in upper division study or during a media internship. It may be evaluated by either faculty or a student's internship supervisor, or both. Other schools may exclude in-

TABLE 20.1
Evaluating Portfolios

| Portfolio Content | Typically Evaluated By | Typical Evaluation Methods |
|---|---|---|
| Work done on internship only | Internship on-site supervisor | On-the job observation or media program's intern evaluation form |
| Internship work plus work done in upper-division courses | Internship on-site supervisor and faculty; perhaps also by local media professional visitors | Same as above plus either faculty's holistic or criterion-referenced evaluation |
| Internship plus work done in all college courses | Internship on-site supervisor and faculty; perhaps also by local media professional visitors | Same as above plus either faculty's holistic or criterion-referenced evaluation |
| Internship, work done in all college courses, plus other on- or off-campus media work | Internship on-site supervisor and faculty, perhaps also by local media professional visitors; also, (possibly) reviews and ratings from on- and off-campus media supervisors | Same as above plus either faculty's holistic or criterion-referenced evaluation and other methods used by on- and off-campus media supervisors |
| Work done in only college courses | Faculty and perhaps local media professional visitors | Faculty's holistic or criterion-referenced evaluation |
| Any combination of the above, plus papers, research projects from "theoretical" courses | Any combination of the personnel listed above | Any combination of the above |

ternship work, limiting the portfolio's contents to media products the student produced during his or her on-campus coursework. Some units use only faculty juries to evaluate their students' portfolios, whereas others impanel a jury of faculty and visiting media professionals. Other schools require, in addition to media products, some evidence of student achievement in the more "theoretical" courses: law, ethics, theory, history, and so forth. Typically, the evidence found in portfolios that assesses student outcomes in these subject areas consists of academic papers or research reports (see Table 20.1).

## DIFFERENT WAYS TO GRADE PORTFOLIOS

Grading methods for portfolios also vary. They include Pass–Fail, letter grades, and numerical scoring. For example, in my department's internship course, which determines the student's final grade by combining an evaluation by the internship supervisor and the student's portfolio score, a numerical score on the portfolio is determined holistically. Three faculty jury members individually score a student's portfolio from 0 to 100, with a score of 70 required to pass. The jury members' scores are averaged and the result is the student's portfolio score. The other half of the student's grade in this internship course is provided by an intern evaluation form filled out by the internship supervisor. This form is also scored from 0 to 100, and the final internship-senior portfolio course grade is determined by averaging these two scores.

Other college and university media programs require the senior portfolio as part of a capstone course. This method is especially popular in units that do not require all of their students to complete an internship.

## WHY PORTFOLIOS?

Why are portfolios becoming popular in media education? Haley and Jackson (1995) called portfolio assessment "authentic," maintaining that this means of assessment ". . . replicates the challenges and standards of performance" encountered in the workplace (p. 30). Many academic units teaching media in the United States—and all that apply for accreditation by the Accrediting Council for Education in Journalism and Mass Communication (ACEJMC)—position themselves in the academic marketplace as professionally oriented. By this they mean that because the majority of undergraduates entering their programs have chosen careers in mass media or as media adjuncts (advertising, public relations, etc.), assessment for such units should determine whether student educational outcomes are sufficient and appropriate for the employment of graduates in the mass media. Evaluating portfolios of student work, especially if this work includes a number of media products, helps faculty and administrators assess such applied outcomes (Donald, 1995).

## WHAT MEDIA BOSSES WANT

Media practitioners constantly remind media educators that the kind of graduates they seek for entry-level positions are those who both write well and are well-versed in the liberal arts and sciences. But media educators also know from experience that employers value graduates most if they can additionally demonstrate competence in the basic practical skills of the profession. (Stone, 1996) Some employers speak in lofty tones about the value of a liberal arts education, but when the time comes to actually hire someone for an entry-level position, the graduate who also knows how to compose a camera shot and edit video, gather the facts and write a news story or news release, or write and create an ad campaign—and has something in hand to show the employer to prove it—will get the job (Steinke, 1993). Including resume tapes, discs, and other evidence in some sort of organized, well-produced portfolio helps students obtain employment. And this one phenomenon assists your unit in another statistic on which you are evaluated: alumni satisfaction surveys.

These days, the typical credentials electronic media graduates bring to the job market are a bachelor's degree in their field plus an eclectic set of experiences collected while working on class projects, campus media, or on an internship or two. Graduates of some mass media programs may also have produced some form of resume tape, or, in more recent years, a multimedia disc, but many lack any proof of ability when they walk across the platform in cap and gown. Media graduates often send out hundreds of cover letters and resumes to potential employers announcing that they are ready, willing, and college-prepared for a job. Sadly, however, few are prepared to provide potential employers with any concrete evidence of their readiness. And employers, many of whom were not top students themselves, are not overly impressed by grades (Cappelli, 1992).

Because the ACEJMC, regional accrediting organizations, and state boards of higher education, now ask or require units to demonstrate assessment of student learning outcomes, and because the portfolio is considered a direct measure, many media educators have chosen to adopt one of the many forms and formats of the portfolio.

## ACEJMC'S EDUCATIONAL OUTCOMES

In recent years, the ACEJMC has codified a list of desired learning outcomes for graduates in journalism and mass communication. The ACEJMC Web site defines them as follows:

Individual professions in journalism and mass communication may require certain specialized values and competencies. Irrespective of their particular specialization, all graduates should be aware of certain core values and competencies and be able to:

- understand and apply the principles and laws of freedom of speech and press, including the right to dissent, to monitor and criticize power, and to assemble and petition for redress of grievances;

- demonstrate an understanding of the history and role of professionals and institutions in shaping communications;
- demonstrate an understanding of the diversity of groups in a global society in relationship to communications;
- understand concepts and apply theories in the use and presentation of images and information;
- demonstrate an understanding of professional ethical principles and work ethically in pursuit of truth, accuracy, fairness and diversity;
- think critically, creatively and independently;
- conduct research and evaluate information by methods appropriate to the communications professions in which they work;
- write correctly and clearly in forms and styles appropriate for the communications professions, audiences and purposes they serve;
- critically evaluate their own work and that of others for accuracy and fairness, clarity, appropriate style and grammatical correctness;
- apply basic numerical and statistical concepts;
- apply tools and technologies appropriate for the communications professions in which they work. (ACEJMC)

Evaluations of intern performance, measured by many units via both intern evaluation instruments and portfolios, cannot always assess every one of these competencies for every intern, especially students interning in advertising, public relations, broadcast production, and other nonjournalistic occupations. But most of the ACEJMC objectives apply to all students, and with the right sort of evaluation form, important assessment data can be acquired from both the internship and the portfolio evaluation. And the use of the portfolio of a student's work produced in classes, campus media, and especially on the job as an intern, helps to holistically evaluate a student's ability to produce media products and conduct research into issues in mass media.

The first ACEJMC competency, relating to a working knowledge of the principles of freedom of speech and press, is encountered daily in journalism interns' efforts to gather and report the news. The mentor–intern relationship between intern and intern supervisor is key to student learning in this area. For example, clips of stories included in their portfolios in which interns were required to deal with government gatekeepers such as the police, the courts, and bureaucrats, might be termed *prima facie* evidence of the extent to which these competencies have been acquired. Likewise, although an understanding of the history and role of professionals and institutions in shaping communications is taught in every classroom in media studies units, the mentor–student relationship reinforces the importance and relevance of key concepts on the job in the "real world," where professionals are constantly working to refine and improve the state of mass communications in America. At least by inference, portfolio content reinforces the unit's confidence in student understanding in this area.

Especially for interns who have had a sheltered upbringing or who have attended colleges in which the student body is not diverse, (e.g., students from rural schools who have not experienced much of the wider world), a well-chosen internship can greatly improve his or her worldview, which helps satisfy the third ACEJMC competency, related to diversity. And, based on student achievement on the internship or in the production of campus student media products, portfolio content reinforces faculty confidence in student understanding of the concepts of diversity.

Assessment results discovered via the use of internship evaluations and portfolios are especially relevant for ACEJMC objective number four, which is concerned with applying theories in the use and presentation of images and information. Examination of portfolio contents produced for campus media or on the internship for utilization of aesthetic, communication, and ethical principles and theories displays a student's practical understanding.

ACEJMC objective number five, an understanding and ability to apply professional ethical principles, is practiced in both campus media and internship work, which will be displayed in the portfolio. The same is true for ACEJMC objective number six, the ability to think critically, creatively, and independently. Media products displayed in portfolios tell the discriminating reader much about the way a student's mind works, how creatively he or she can convey the information, and whether he or she derived facts and values independently or lazily relied on less-than-objective "official" sources.

Not all items included in a portfolio help to assess ACEJMC objective number six, the ability to conduct research and evaluate information by methods appropriate to the communications professions in which communications practitioners work. Certainly the student journalist, both in campus media work and on the internship, can easily demonstrate this trait in the content of his or her portfolio. But some media products, such as those developed while working in the creative services side of advertising, producing commercials, and so forth, do not lend themselves easily to display of competency in this objective.

However, the seventh ACEJMC competency, to write correctly and clearly in forms and styles appropriate for the communications professions, is very clearly shown in media products created for campus media and internships and displayed in the portfolio. This is extremely helpful in faculty assessment activities.

The eighth objective, a student's ability to critically evaluate his or her work, is one in which the portfolio is perhaps the best indicator. One of the important skills derived from the compilation of one's work in a portfolio is the ability to judge the quality of the items chosen for inclusion versus those that are inferior and should be left out. An added bonus in learning by repetition occurs when the student judges a media product he or she produced to be unsatisfactory and rewrites or reedits it to make it acceptable.

Objective number nine, applying basic numerical and statistical concepts, is mostly relevant to the journalism or public relations students who must, for example, examine and report on research content or create factoids in newspaper and magazine stories for their internships or for campus media. Advertising campaign proposals and other such items produced for class projects and internship work also make use of quantitative methods and can be included in portfolios to demonstrate competency.

It is easy to see how ACEJMC objective number 10, a student's ability to apply tools and technologies appropriate for the communications professions in which he or she works, is best gauged via the portfolio. Student campus media productions and media products produced on the internships are again prima facie evidence.

## TWO UNIVERSITIES' PORTFOLIO PROGRAMS

In 1991, as chair of the Department of Communications at the University of Tennessee at Martin (UT-Martin), and again in 1998, as chair of the Department of Mass Communications at Southern Illinois University at Edwardsville (SIUE), I lead my faculty through the process of developing portfolio assessment for our units (see the Appendix). They adopted a senior portfolio as the official graded exit test requirement for all communications majors. Scores of 0 to 100 were possible, but a score of 70 was required to graduate. A student who failed to achieve a 70 could resubmit a revised portfolio after either its contents were revised or enlarged, or, in an unusual case, the student completed additional coursework or practicum experience.

At UT-Martin, the faculty hoped that because a satisfactory portfolio score would be required to pass the Senior Seminar and thus qualify for graduation, and because students would perceive the end product as worthwhile, portfolio assessment might provide more valid assessment plus significantly improved programmatic feedback. Then, portfolio-in-hand, students would leave the university with a professionally prepared, persuasive "sales brochure" to assist them in the job search. And because achievement of a satisfactory portfolio score required them to produce more quality media products while enrolled in the program, students, through additional or repeated learning experiences, would hopefully become more adept at the skills of the profession.

Likewise, in 1997, the faculty of SIUE were in search of a new capstone experience for their students. As an institution, SIUE requires each undergraduate to complete a "senior project." Each department is responsible for providing students with the requirements for the project. The faculty adopted the senior portfolio as their senior project. Unlike UT-Martin, which folded the portfolio requirement into the capstone course, SIUE's portfolio is part of the department's required internship course.

## BORROWING FROM THE ARTS

Senior portfolio requirements command student notice by asking them to demonstrate a certain standard of holistic competence before they are permitted to graduate. Borrowing from the jury system used to assess the synthesis of learning and skills in the disciplines of music, art, and theatre, faculty believe that the quality of the media products that students have learned to create (e.g., radio news stories, scripts, TV commercials, public service announcements [PSAs], press releases, TV programs, multimedia presentations, etc.) holistically represent the educational objectives of the entire professionally oriented curricula better than any other single evaluative measure.

## WHETHER TO USE PROFESSIONAL JUDGES

A faculty jury system for portfolios is common. But some programs also utilize local media professionals as part of the jury process. One reason many colleges and universities do not choose to use working pros in portfolio assessment is because of the structure or complexity of the department's curriculum. In the case of SIUE, the portfolio requirement is combined with an internship. Faculty know the students, know their work in their courses, and wish to judge student work—and student progress—themselves. Because SIUE's internship evaluation process involves intern supervisors separately judging the work the students have accomplished on the job, both academic and working professional review of student competencies are utilized. (See a copy of this form at the end of this chapter. It includes many questions posed by the faculty as well as the ACEJMC's educational objectives.) So, both the professional in the workplace and the professors who have taught the students for 4 years evaluate evidence of student achievement from their particular perspectives.

On many campuses, portfolio assessment has generated a positive qualitative ripple effect. But there are also problem areas. The remainder of this chapter discusses some of the advantages and disadvantages and provides a close-up of how the senior portfolio has been operationalized at SIUE over the last 6 years.

## ADVANTAGES OF THE PORTFOLIO

• Faculty members actively support the portfolio requirement in all their courses, identifying in their syllabi which course projects are appropriate for students to save for their senior portfolios.

• As a result, faculty report a surprising benefit: Before they required senior portfolios, instructors would, for example, pass back a student's script assignment for a radio commercial, marked up with the usual amount of red pen. Ninety-nine times out of a hundred, after class was dismissed, that script would end up in a trash can in the hallway. But now the student, who knows that this project is a possible portfolio element, not only saves his or her work, but also reads the professor's criticism more carefully, makes corrections to the original, and, if he or she is cautious, saves it on both hard copy and disc for the portfolio. So, as an advertising practitioner might phrase it, requiring portfolios provides professors with "more bang for the buck" in each class assignment.

• Faculty can periodically review the success of the individual objectives within each course they teach in light of the competencies displayed by students in their portfolios. Then, as a committee, faculty within each sequence can assess how these objectives work together.

• Some faculty give their students extra course credit for "miniportfolios"—final compilations of student work throughout the semester in a single course. Assignments are rewritten, reshot, or reedited to reflect the improvements on the original assignments suggested by their professors. In describing the use of miniportfolios for courses, McClelland (1991) made the case that there is another implicit advantage: changing the student culture from a goal of doing work to get a grade for a course to "getting it right," focusing on "texts, readers, revision, development and potential—not on grades" (pp. 165–173).

• Because of this more mature focus, students seem to take their classes and their class projects more seriously, because they are later required to display a heightened competence by revising and improving their work for their portfolios. They must actually master the new skills assigned rather than just complete projects: Learning becomes the goal, not just collecting grades and credits.

• Students volunteer for work at campus media outlets. They "stay with it" until they master the skills. Becker, Kosicki, Engleman, and Viswanath (1993) said that success in the job market is much more likely for those with significant experience in campus media.

• Students seem more confident in their ability to compete for jobs after preparing a portfolio: They know they can do professional-quality work because they have a juried portfolio to prove it. Through this process, students also learn another valuable job skill: evaluating their own work, culling through their accomplishments, choosing and polishing their very best—also demonstrating to potential employers that they know quality work when they see it (Forrest, 1990; Hutchings, 1990).

• Because the faculty in each sequence sit on juries together to evaluate portfolios, they learn more about what their colleagues are doing in the classroom and what they're assigning. Redundancy in the curriculum is reduced through enhanced faculty communication. At all levels of education, portfolios are used—and praised—for the feedback they provide those who teach (Schilling & Schilling, 1993).

• Faculty also can more easily evaluate the results of courses that build on each other.

• Identifying uniform weaknesses among graduating seniors prompts faculty to alter course content or create new curriculum or requirements.

• These last two benefits are significant. Student course evaluation survey forms tell faculty little about what students have actually learned in a course: in this sense, they really only tell a professor what students liked or didn't like about the course units he or she taught. Correct his or her assignment, give out a grade, but what can the student really do, what has he or she been able to synthesize when finishing a course? But look at an end-of-semester miniportfolio assignment and one can readily see if the student really "got it." Evaluate that same student's portfolio as a graduating senior and faculty can more easily track a student's overall improvement, increased sophistication, and ability to judge the quality of their own work.

• And when faculty see the results of their efforts in context with the rest of a student's learning experiences and achievements, they can more easily pinpoint programmatic strengths and weaknesses. For example, if faculty members meet around a table to evaluate senior portfolios, discussion often leads to alterations in both course and curriculum content. After changes have been in place for a period of time, faculty can evaluate effectiveness in subsequent portfolios. For example, after a few years of evaluating what they considered to be the substandard writing in Television-Radio student portfolios at SIUE, the Television-Radio faculty created a new course to anchor the sequence, Advanced Broadcast Writing. In subsequent years' portfolios, Television-Radio student writing improved.

It is clear to UT-Martin and SIUE faculty how advantageous portfolios are to the success of their programs. Potential employers have been impressed as well. Many graduates have reported that the statement on their resume regarding the availability of a portfolio has prompted many employers to ask to see them. Graduates are advised to use this request as an excuse to visit the station, newspaper office, public relations firm, and so forth, and deliver the portfolio in person to get "face time"—one additional chance to make a positive impression.

## DISADVANTAGES OF THE PORTFOLIO

No evaluation system is perfect, and portfolio assessment has potential pitfalls to consider:

• The most frequently cited concern with portfolios is the issue of authenticity. How can you be sure that students are turning in their own work? If students' professors evaluate the portfolios, there is little concern about that. Professors are well aware of whose work they are seeing, sometimes for the third or fourth time. This is key to the authenticity issue: The same professors who have assigned, evaluated, graded, and sometimes reevaluated the same work again in miniportfolios at the end of the semester are the persons judging these final senior portfolios. In a system such as this, there is little problem with student dishonesty. Later on in this chapter, read how SIUE's portfolio instructions deal with claiming only the portion of a group project a student actually produced.

• Rudner (1992) discussed a typology of rater effects that can skew the results of portfolio assessment. They include the following:

  a. "The halo effect," in which positive or negative prior impressions about a particular student may color faculty jury evaluation of the portfolio.

  b. "Stereotyping," in which faculty juries may unfairly consider entire groups of students as possessing certain characteristics. For example, the SIUE faculty have always considered print journalism students to be the best writers in the department. This may skew evaluations of writing upward for these students.

c. "Perception differences," in which the viewpoints and past experiences of an evaluator can affect how he or she interprets behavior (or student-produced media products).

d. "Leniency or stringency error"—When viewing another professor's assignment in a portfolio, a colleague may not "have enough knowledge to make an objective rating," resulting in "scores that are systematically higher or lower."

e. "Scale shrinking"—"Some judges will not use the end of any scale."

As valuable as portfolios are to assessment in a professional media program, it is important to note that it is not enough to rely completely on portfolio evaluation. As introduced earlier, if internships are required in the media program, students should also be evaluated by their professional mentors.

To provide extra assurance that solid learning is taking place on internships, students should evaluate their experiences in "internship papers," detailing their learning experiences while on internship. In addition, at SIUE, under the same internship course rubric, students also are required to evaluate their own experience in their mass communications studies via anonymous graduating senior assessment letters.


## SHARED PURPOSE

It should be reemphasized that to be successful, any assessment plan must meet both the corporate evaluative needs of the sponsoring department and the self-evaluative needs of each student. As Banta (1993) put it, the preeminent task is to "build a sense of shared purpose among students, faculty, and administrators based on clearly articulated and communicated statements of mission and educational goals" (p. 3).

Helen Barrett (2000), in writing on her Web site about electronic teacher portfolios, nonetheless described a series of qualities that are particular to any exceptional portfolio. Aiming a portfolio program for these goals will ensure that over time, student learning, the ability to demonstrate learning, and overall student success, will improve if their portfolios

a. possess a high level of thought;
b. are polished;
c. demonstrate considerable effort;
d. are thorough;
e. are well-organized;

f.  show a variety of products;

g.  are unique;

h.  demonstrate substantial application to their career goals;

i.  shows the individual's personality;

j.  demonstrates both breath and depth;

k.  are highly imaginative. (Barrett, 2000)

## SUMMARY

To sum up, one can only add that portfolio assessment of the kind described here serves the combined objectives of a holistic measure of student achievement, encourages student participation in active learning, provides a once-per-semester outcome evaluation of a department's curriculum and course content, gives the faculty another way to gauge the success of their efforts and delivers a valid, direct assessment of applied student learning. And for the students, the end result is a portfolio that they can also use to assist them in obtaining employment.

In 1992, when I first researched portfolio assessment, I was interested with the diversity of methods and uses that I encountered in elementary and secondary education. To end this chapter, I would like to suggest that readers acquaint themselves with this literature:

- http://ericec.org/osep/newsbriefs/news17.html (Alternative uses of portfolios for students with disabilities).
- http://www.teachervision.fen.com/lesson-plans/lesson-4528.html? detoured= (Pros and cons of portfolios for teachers and students. Note: You must register your e-mail address to access this site, but you may opt out of receiving any e-mail back from them).
- http://electronicportfolios.org/portfolios.html (Using technology to create and evaluate portfolios. This Web site also lists the URLs of a number of other helpful and interesting sites).
- http://www.degreeinfo.com/article23_1.html (This is an article, "Portfolio Assessment in Higher Education: Seeking Credibility on the Campus").
- http://ag.arizona.edu/fcs/cyfernet/cyfar/Portfo~3.htm (This in-depth discussion covers a considerable amount of ground, including strengths and weaknesses, practice and procedure).
- http://reading.indiana.edu/ieo/bibs/portfoli.html (An excellent bibliography on portfolios, including other Web sites).

# REFERENCES

Accrediting Council for Education in Journalism and Mass Communication. (2003). *Policies of Accreditation*. Retrieved July 12, 2005, from http://www.ku.edu/~acejmc/PROGRAM/POLICIES.SHTML#elig

Accrediting Council for Education in Journalism and Mass Communication. (2003). *Principles of Accreditation*. Retrieved July 12, 2005, from http://www.ku.edu/~acejmc/PROGRAM/PRINCIPLES.SHTML

Banta, T. W. (Ed.). (1993). *Making a difference: Outcomes of a decade of assessment in higher education.* San Francisco: Jossey-Bass.

Barrett, H. C. (2000). *Electronic portfolios = multimedia development + portfolio development: The electronic portfolio development process.* Retrieved from http:electronicportfolios.org

Becker, L. B., Kosicki, T., Engleman, T., & Viswanath, K. (1993). Finding work and getting paid: Predictors of success in the mass communications job market. *Journalism Quarterly, 70,* 919–933.

Cappelli, P. (1992). College, students and the workplace: Assessing performance to improve the fit. *Change,* 54–58.

Cohen, J. (2004). Editor's note: Assessment . . . yours, mine and ours. *Journalism and Mass Communication Educator, 59,* 3–5.

Donald, R. (1995). The senior portfolio: Assessment with a ripple effect. *Feedback, 36*(2), 13–16.

Forrest, A. (1990). Time will tell: Portfolio-assisted assessment of general education. *Report of the American Association for Higher Education Assessment Forum,* 18–24.

Haley, E., & Jackson, D. (1995). A conceptualization of assessment for mass communication programs. *Journalism and Mass Communication Educator, 50,* 26–34.

Hutchings, P. (1990, April). Learning over time: Portfolio assessment. *AAHE Bulletin,* pp. 6–8.

Larson, R. L. (1991). Using portfolios in the assessment of writing in the academic disciplines. In P. Belanoff & M. Dickson (Eds.), *Portfolios: Process and product* (pp. 137–149). Portsmouth, NH: Boynton/Cook.

McClelland, K. (1991). Portfolios: Solution to a problem. In P. Belanoff & M. Dickson (Eds.), *Portfolios: Process and product* (pp. 165–173). Portsmouth, NH: Boynton/Cook.

Rudner, L. M. (1992). Reducing errors due to the use of judges. *Practical Assessment, Research and Evaluation.* Retrieved from http://pareonline.net/getvn.asp?v= 3&n=3

Schilling, K. M., & Schilling, K. L. (1993). Professors must respond to calls for accountability. *Chronicle of Higher Education, XXXIX,* A-40.

Steinke, G. (1993). Tennessee broadcasters prefer workers with college communications training. *Feedback, 34*(1), 7–9.

Stone, V. (1996). *News directors favor hands-on schools.* Retrieved from http://www.missouri.edu/~jourvs/ndprefs.html

Vavrus, L. (1990). Putting portfolios to the test. *Instructor, 100,* 48–53.

# APPENDIX

## Example of Portfolio Requirements

What follows is an abridged version of Southern Illinois University at Edwardsville's (SIUE) handout for students, describing the department's senior portfolio requirements. The entire text, including content requirements for each of SIUE's sequences, is available by e-mailing the author at rdonald@siue.edu:

*MC 481 Senior Portfolio Instructions*
For academic year 2003–2004, revised Spring, 2004
Southern Illinois University Edwardsville

The senior portfolio is a compilation of the best coursework and projects you have produced while in college. A portfolio can also include media products you've produced at other colleges before you transferred to SIUE, work you've produced during your internship or in professional media jobs while in college. Detailed further below are instructions on how to compile your senior portfolio.

## Portfolio Instructions

The immediate purpose of the portfolio is to demonstrate to a jury of department faculty in your professional option what you have learned to do well during your time here, and whether or not you are ready to graduate. But portfolios also have another valuable and practical purpose for you: When you graduate, you cannot expect to be hired as a professional communicator (especially in this competitive job market) if you can't prove that you can do the work—and do it better than all those other mass communications graduates with whom you're competing. As this department's faculty has stressed throughout your time here, the well-laid-out contents of a Mass Communications Department graduate's published clips or photos, Ad/P.R. portfolio, multimedia CD or resume/audition tape plus writing samples could be that extra bit of evidence that will make a potential employer choose you over other applicants.

If for one reason or another, you may not now possess all the items you need, don't panic! There's still time to join the staff of the *Alestle* [campus newspaper] or WSIE-FM, etc., this semester—produce a lot, and save everything. To help you understand what we're talking about, here are a few examples of portfolio materials you can collect from your coursework, your work at WSIE, the *Alestle* and other campus publications (e.g., the *Mass Communicator,* [department alumni magazine]), and from your work while on internship or part-time media-related jobs. Also, faculty members should tell you in your classes what course assignments and projects you should keep (and improve upon) for inclusion in your portfolio.

Below are *examples* of some of the items you can include in your portfolio. Please note that these are not inclusive lists, just some examples. See your adviser or the internship coordinator if you have any questions.

- Radio production/news air checks and television production/news resume tapes;
- Other tapes, or excerpts from tapes of radio or television programs or program elements you produced;
- Any broadcast copy (news, continuity, commercials, documentaries—any kind of script or treatment/story outline used for broadcast or corporate communications). Regarding style, this department's web site *<www.siue.edu/MASSCOMM>* contains script format models (eg., 2-column TV commercial script, radio news script, 8½ × 11 TV storyboard, WGA film-style script, WGA Treatment/Story Outline format etc.), which are used by faculty in teaching all courses [in our curriculum]. These comprise the default department standards for each kind of script. All scripts in your portfolios must precisely conform to these formats. NOTE: If scripts you write on your internship require a different style—which is quite likely—that's OK. Put this work in a separate section in your portfolio and identify the section as, for example, "News Copy: KMOX Internship." But all copy written here at SIUE should conform to department style.
- Professionally oriented class projects and reports (ad campaign presentations, media plans, pitches, research reports, legal briefs);
- Multimedia CDs, web pages, photography, etc. (NOTE: Some web sites should be included on a disc (or on discs) in your portfolio. Others will work better for presentation if you make good 8½ × 11 color laser prints of these web pages and insert the prints into a special section in your portfolio. Ask your multimedia professor for advice on yours. But one thing is sure: you should never just refer the reader to an URL. The overriding strategy of this portfolio is to make reading it a convenient, enjoyable experience for the potential employer);
- Clippings of any of your published stories and/or photos in any print media;
- Newspaper, magazine or any publication page layouts you have designed;
- News, feature, op-ed pieces and other copy written for class assignments;
- Ad, P.R. or corporate copy, media kits and storyboards;
- Any work similar to the above that you have produced while working in the professional media and/or on your internship.

Finally, the last section of your portfolio should demonstrate for the MassComm faculty what you have accomplished in research, critical thinking, and your ability to apply theory in some form of scholarly inquiry. You have written a number of research papers to satisfy the requirements of the courses you have completed for the Mass Communications major. You can also use papers for courses outside the major that are MassComm-related. Include at least three of these papers in this section. Any research papers you may have presented at academic or professional conferences could certainly be included. Since many of these papers are of some length, it is suggested that you do not enclose each page in plastic, as you will for all of your other work. Instead, when you purchase your portfolio binder, choose one with pockets in the front and back. So, for example, you can place your resume tape in the front pocket and your term papers in the back pocket.

*Note*: Always remove instructor comments, grades, errors noted, etc., from anything you plan to put in your portfolio. Any copy, paper, project or assignment worthy of inclusion in your portfolio should be re-printed after you re-edit, sharpen and fix it. Now that you're ready to graduate, you should be much more experienced and knowledgeable than you were when you wrote these pieces. So rewrite them! Never show off your mistakes to potential employers or to the faculty jury that will review your portfolio: always put your best foot forward. If you don't present your best work now, when you're selling yourself as an entry-level professional to our faculty and potential employers, when will you? And if getting a job isn't enough of a practical reason, consider this: more than one faculty member penalize a student's score one point for every single instance of incorrect spelling, typographical or style error. Get the picture?

*Also Note*: Many kinds of class project materials require introductory explanations. Sometimes it's because the item or the project/campaign materials won't make complete sense to a potential employer unless you provide some context for them. Also, if you contributed a part of a group project, include in your portfolio only the part of the project that you produced. When you're displaying your portion of any group project, communicate! Put the whole project in context by preceding it with a tabbed section divider, plus an introductory page. In this introduction, describe the entire project, explain the different parts of the project, and then state clearly just what you personally contributed to the project. Then the pages that follow will make sense to a potential employer. Speaking of those tabbed sections, make the tabs look professional: make them printed tabs, never hand-lettered. Hand-lettering is unprofessional.

If you're having trouble deciding what to leave in and what to leave out, ask your faculty adviser or the internship coordinator for advice.

# The Capstone Course

Robert C. Moore
*Department of Communications*
*Elizabethtown College*

In examining a basis for the existence of a capstone course, the literature in the field of Education, specifically Curriculum and Instruction,
provides some direction. From a wide variety of definitions for curriculum, a definition by Hilda Taba seems particularly useful because it
specifies the elements of curriculum:

> A curriculum usually contains a statement of aims and of specific objec-
> tives; it indicates some selection and organization of content; it either im-
> plies or manifests certain patterns of learning and teaching, whether be-
> cause the objectives demand them or because the content organization
> requires them. Finally, it includes a program of evaluation of the out-
> comes. (Oliva, 1982, p. 7)

These elements are not mutually exclusive. Their integration should result in a positive and successful learning experience. The critical last element, evaluation, not only validates the learning, but also enables faculty to revise and refine courses or curricula to continually attain desired
outcomes. Just as curriculum development is a systematic process, curriculum evaluation is a systematic process by which the students' total
education is weighed.

Outcomes assessment must be systematic. Schools are called on not
only by academic and political demands but also by the very ethics that
underlie the profession, to develop numerous direct and indirect measures of student learning to provide both proof and accountability that

higher education is accomplishing those things that are specified by it as important. Volkwein (2003) suggested that a systematic plan of outcomes assessment gives appropriateness to the mission statement, utility of the institutional goals and objectives, adequacy of assessment measures, and the impact of programs on students.

In 2003, the Accrediting Council on Education in Journalism and Mass Communication (ACEJMC) adopted a revision of accreditation standards. Regardless of a school's desire to undergo accreditation, these standards provide a useful academic foundation for curriculum design and development recognized nationally. Standard 2, in particular, deals with curriculum design and stresses specific expectations that are to be included in courses of study. Standard 9 is applicable in that it sets out numerous expectations for student learning. Incorporation of several of these expectations into a curriculum also requires that they are able to be assessed.

The capstone course is an excellent method of direct assessment. By its very nature, the capstone course is a method of summative evaluation. It not only assesses previous cognitive learning in the major, but also provides a forum that allows an instructor to assesses the student's overall collegiate learning experience. Because, in addition to cognitive skills, learning can occur in two other domains (affective and psychomotor), a capstone course allows for a mix of evaluative styles that assess the broad range of the students' past experiences (Kemp & Smellie, 1989, p. 20). This approach also allows a student, who perhaps excels in one area more than another, to demonstrate the strengths of his or her learning. Achievement in the cognitive domain is usually represented by an ability to recall, understand, and apply knowledge. Evaluation of affective learning is characterized by expression of feelings, values, and attitudes (especially regarding events, issues, and topics related to, or impacting, the students' field of study). Finally, psychomotor learning is evaluated by the application and performance of skills. Ideally, a student's competence will be satisfactorily demonstrated in all three learning modalities.

In a summative evaluation of the students' experience in the university curriculum, a capstone course is an instrument used to directly assess the performance of students in the attainment of institutional and departmental curricular expectations. Additionally, it provides the opportunity to address and assess the relevant accrediting standards and those of professional bodies. It is an in-depth opportunity for the student to demonstrate accomplishment of the full spectrum of that learning. A useful model for such expectations is Bloom's (1956) *A Taxonomy of Educational Objectives.* These progressive levels of objectives are as follows: recall of knowledge, comprehension, application, analysis, synthesis, and evaluation. The last three levels are higher order intellectual activity. They are concerned more with the how and why of learning rather than the what.

Affective learning has been referred to by Bloom (1971) as the implicit curriculum (p. 14). It is made up of attitudes, interests, values, and feelings derived by the student through learning and by interaction with other learners and professors. The affective domain of learning advanced by David Krathwohl (Kemp, 1975) consists of five levels: receiving, responding, valuing, organization, and characterization of a value complex. This final level, the highest order, indicates that one's beliefs, ideas, and attitudes have been integrated into a total professional philosophy.

Psychomotor learning is an ongoing refinement process. Such learning is assessed as units and courses are completed. Often, new courses bring with them different and unusual forms of learning. For example, an oral performance course may develop voice delivery to a more refined stage whereas a course in interpretation may require a new application of that previously learned skill. A course in video production may require the development of an unfamiliar combination and synchronization of finely coordinated movements. Psychomotor learning encompasses gross bodily movements, finely coordinated movements, nonverbal communication, and speech behaviors (Kemp, 1975).

The capstone course expectations should be a display of a mastery of all three modalities of learning and the ability to apply them to new, unusual, and integrated project requirements. Table 21.1 specifies the pro-

TABLE 21.1
Learning Expectations in a Capstone Course

| Learning Modality | Course Expectations |
|---|---|
| Cognitive Learning | |
| Recall of knowledge | Students are presented with a problem and draw on |
| Comprehension | their knowledge and research to weigh and select |
| Application | various data leading to a solution of the problem |
| Analysis | which is workable and intellectually defensible. |
| Synthesis | |
| Evaluation | |
| Affective Learning | |
| Receiving | The approach and decisions made reflect attitudes, |
| Responding | values, feelings, and beliefs characteristic of the |
| Valuing | discipline and the profession. |
| Organization | |
| Value complex | |
| Psychomotor Learning | |
| Gross bodily movements | The production of a project which serves as a solu- |
| Finely coordinated movements | tion to a problem and the oral and visual presen- |
| | tation of it. |
| Nonverbal communication | Both reflect a degree of skill and competency as a |
| Speech behaviors | communicator. |

gressive levels of achievement in each of the learning modalities and the expectations of student performance in a capstone course.

Other learning theories have been advanced that present reinforcing views of the three domains of learning. Kemp and Smellie (1989) cited Gagné in clarifying the hierarchical structure of learning and also noted that learning is a

> cumulative process. Basic information or simple skills . . . contribute to the learning of more complex knowledge and skills. [Gagné] identified five categories of learning: verbal information, intellectual skills, cognitive strategies, motor skills, and attitudes . . . These [also] fall into three phases of learning advanced by Bell-Gredler: preparation for learning, acquisition and performance, and retrieval and transfer [of knowledge, attitudes and skills]. (Kemp & Smellie, 1989, p. 16)

Kemp and Smellie (1989) also noted that Merrill classifies outcomes of learning in two dimensions. First, content is drawn from advancing levels of facts, concepts, procedures, and principles. The second outcome of learning is performance characterized by remembering, using, and finding a generality.

These approaches to learning provide a basis for course design and evaluation. Learning expectations of students should increase with their advancement through a curriculum. A capstone course might be designed that makes use of the increasing complexity of student learning when the end of the process of instruction is reached. The course uses cumulative learning, after all previous courses and objectives have been met, to relate to more than a single concept; the course draws on the whole of the learning experience and requires that it be applied in a meaningful way.

## OUTCOMES ASSESSMENT AND THE CAPSTONE COURSE

For too long, university curricula have seemed to be too specialized and fragmented. More often than not, students plodded from one course to another and often were provided little opportunity to link the relevant content and skills across the various courses. The role of the capstone course is to draw all of that learning together and to provide a single opportunity or experience during which a student demonstrates that he or she has accomplished or achieved congruence with the university and department's educational goals as represented by the appropriate mission statements and courses taken (Volkwein, 2003).

Unfortunately, faculty often see few links between their courses and those of colleagues in other departments. The learning acquired by stu-

8. Leadership capacity is exhibiting the capacity to contribute as a productive member of the profession and assuming appropriate leadership roles.

9. Scholarly concern for improvement is recognizing the need to increase knowledge and to advance the profession through both theoretical and applied research.

10. Motivation of continued learning is exploring and expanding personal, civic, and professional knowledge and skills through a lifetime. (Blanchard & Christ, 1993, pp. 15–16)

The outcomes specified in the Michigan report and several of those specified in ACEJMC Standards 2 and 9, by Newton (n.d., p. 1), or those drawn from the proceedings of The Senior Year Experience and Students in Transition conference (Cuseo, 1998, p. 22), provide a blueprint for higher education—a benchmark by which institutional and departmental mission statements might be based. Table 21.2 lists many of these outcomes expectations and indicates how they can be categorized into one or more of the modalities of learning previously discussed.

## MISSION STATEMENTS AND A RATIONALE
## FOR THE CAPSTONE COURSE

An American Association of Higher Education (AAHE, n.d.) document on assessment notes that it is most effective when it [is] multidimen-

TABLE 21.2
Integrating Expected Outcomes With the Modalities of Learning

| | Cognitive Learning | Affective Learning | Psychomotor Learning |
|---|---|---|---|
| Communication Competence (written, spoken, mediated) | X | | X |
| Critical Thinking | X | X | |
| Contextual Competence (concepts, theories) | X | X | |
| Aesthetic or Creative Competence | | X | X |
| Professional Roles and Ethics | | X | |
| Adaptive Competence | X | X | X |
| Leadership Capacity (ability to be independent) | | X | |
| Scholarly Concern for Improvement (evaluation) | X | X | |
| Motivation for Continued Learning | X | X | |
| Research Capacity | X | | |

sional, integrated ... with explicitly stated purposes ... which illuminate questions that people really care about ... which lead to improvement [and] promote[s] change.

The capstone course may be the singular opportunity to determine if the student has assimilated the various goals of his or her total education. "The purpose [of the capstone course] ... should be defined in light of each institution's purposes (B. L. Smith, 1998, p. 90). It can be a self-directed, integrated, learning opportunity with goals established on several levels. The first and most global in nature are the general goals of higher education which have been represented here as those articulated by the Michigan Report, AAHE, and others. They tend to be written as societal goals for higher education. Based on these broad statements of outcomes, the university and department design their mission statements using the philosophical approach to education most congruent with that campus' culture and direction of that particular department. These statements of outcomes are the linchpins on which capstone courses are taught. They provide the focus for expectations in the capstone course (see chapter 3).

Each academic department, in successfully formulating a mission statement, makes an attempt to draw into its goals those of higher education and those of the educational institution. Yet, given the varied focuses possible in any discipline, especially communications, the institution perspective is refined in the departmental document. Articulation of goals at this level is vital. Here, the profile of the educated individual is specified. It is that profile, and the level of attainment of it, which is critical in an outcomes assessment, in particular, the capstone course.

Murphy (2003, p. 1) cited a rationale for capstone courses by Wagenaar (1993). Key objectives that should be demonstrated by the student are:

1. Integrating and synthesizing the field;
2. Extending the field;
3. Critiquing the field;
4. Applying the field;
5. Addressing issues raised in ... introductory course(s), but at a higher level;
6. Exploring key arguments in the field;
7. Making connections with general education;
8. Specific comparisons with other fields;
9. Critically thinking generally and within the field;
10. Examining values and views of life.

Kings College (1986) saw these objectives as being able to be articulated in what it referred to as "transferable skills." They are the skills a student masters throughout his or her learning and through which he or she communicates attainment of the course goal. They are "critical thinking, creative thinking and problem solving strategies, effective writing, effective oral communication, quantitative analysis, computer literacy, library competency, . . . [research methods, and skills in mediated communication]" (Kings College, 1986, p. 23). Alverno College faculty developed similar expectations as they defined an educated person (B. L. Smith, 1998).

In a study by Lockhart and Borland (2001), faculty ranked the relative importance of several of these items for inclusion in a capstone course. Ninety-one percent of the faculty surveyed rated "thinking effectively" as the most major in importance in a capstone course. Other elements that were important included "using complex knowledge in making decisions and judgment" (82%), "exercise and expand intellectual curiosity" (67%), "develop skills (as) life-long learners" (64%), "write effectively" (53%), and "think across areas of specialization and integrate ideas from a variety of . . . disciplines and applied fields" (53%) (p. 21).

At Elizabethtown College, the attainment of many institutional goals is incorporated into the course expectations as are the goals and objectives of the departmental mission statement. These documents also incorporate either directly or indirectly select ACEJMC expectations and those of several professional associations. Although not all of these outcomes may be appropriate in all communication curricula, requirements of the capstone course provide a means through which a faculty member may judge a student's performance against those outcomes. (The institutional and departmental mission statements referred to here can be found on the author's homepage under Research, Capstone Course, at: http://users.etown.edu/m/moorerc/).

The capstone course at Elizabethtown College is broader than courses with similar purposes at other institutions. Depending on the nature of those communication programs, capstone courses may be more or less specialized to provide outcomes assessment appropriate to the department's mission.

## DESIGN OF THE COMMUNICATIONS CAPSTONE COURSE

Levine (1998) reported that only two-fifths of colleges and universities have employed the capstone approach. Henscheid's (2000) research has shown that most capstone courses are in the major. They often require a project and a presentation but those that require a thesis tend to be at small selective schools. The focus of the capstone should be to design an experience that integrates the discipline and the liberal arts. Further, it also creates an environment to assess a variety of skills seen as important in higher education. A student as a "compleat" communicator must be able to meet the competencies set out by the institution and the department. If skills development is a part of the curriculum, demonstration of abilities must go beyond "nuts and bolts." Faculty expectations are that students will use their knowledge and the information gathered to plan, design, and produce original projects that integrate various types of expression. Such expectations provide a basis, indeed a mandate, for a capstone course that can adequately assess such learning. Blanchard and Christ (1993) called this approach "cross-training . . . a flexible, fundamental, integrated approach to media education . . ." (p. 32).

Learning, not teaching, is at the center of capstone experiences. Redmond (1998) said that "breadth of understanding . . . [and] depth of abilities" are key aspects to evaluating summary learning (p. 74). Such courses are student-centered and seldom resemble those in traditional classrooms. Problem analysis, information sharing, creative solutions, and projects drive the capstone course. Student expression is critical to demonstrating successful achievement of capstone course objectives. The professor should be a mentor and guide, a consultant or counselor.

The capstone course, as presented here, is based on applied research. Students presented with a new problem must utilize their knowledge, experience, and abilities to plan and research various solutions to the problem and then correctly apply the chosen solution as an effective way to meet the purpose and goal of the problem. Multifaceted problems present challenges to the student that require the use of knowledge gained in divergent courses. Focusing that knowledge in a single capstone course provides the opportunity for applied research to meet varied demands. Additionally, in professionally oriented programs, when "real-world" problems are presented, then it is valuable that students work with "real-world" clients in developing solutions. This practical-experiential component allows the student to begin to develop a sense of professional identity by working with individuals already in the field and jointly developing a meaningful project (see chapter 17).

Glaser and Radliff (2000) called such a task or real problem a service learning experience and that its inclusion is critical to a communication capstone course. For students moving on to graduate school, systematic research and its application provides excellent background and experience. The course begins a transition from school to an eventual career as the students work closely with clients and actively draw on past learning. The benefits of such an evolution include the practice of adaptive competence, establishment of the beginnings of a professional identity, observation of professional ethics, and utilizing learning within the context of one's living and working environment—all key outcomes previously cited as critical to higher education.

## THE CAPSTONE COURSE GOAL

The departmental and institutional mission statements, incorporating various elements and the spirit of the Carnegie report, the Michigan report, and authors Andreasen and Trede (1998), Carlson and Peterson (1993), Smith (1993), and others, provide a basis for the direction and development of curriculum at the institutional and departmental level. They also provide for a basis on which a capstone course goal might be formulated. One such goal statement for the course might be as follows: "The capstone course is a culminating experience that integrates coursework, knowledge, skills, and experiential learning to enable the student to demonstrate a broad mastery of specialized learning with that from across the curriculum for a promise of initial employability and further learning and career advancement."

## THE CAPSTONE COURSE REQUIREMENTS

The Carnegie Foundation recommends three instruments for measuring outcomes in a capstone course. These include the following: a senior thesis (which draws on the historical, social, and ethical perspectives of the major), an oral presentation of the thesis with peer critique, and preparation of a portfolio (see chapter 20); ("Prologue and Major Recommendations," 1986). Volkwein (2003) concurred that outcomes assessment requires multiple measures of student learning (p. 4). The capstone course at Elizabethtown College requires four instruments to measure outcomes.

### The Senior Thesis

The thesis examines the history, values, ethics, and social perspectives of the discipline related to a particular problem or issue. The research study extends the prior knowledge of the student through the conducting of a literature review. The student then proceeds to conceptualize the study, develop procedures, analyze the data, and make recommendations regarding the topic or problem.

## The Senior Project

Students in professional or performance-based curricula might be required to produce a project specifically tied to the thesis. The purpose of the project is to provide an opportunity for the research work to actually be a workable solution to the problem presented. Production or performance at this level not only demonstrates applied skills and abilities but also allows for practically applied research.

The projects that are selected ". . . follow three major guidelines. First, the student should believe that there is a substantial need for the project. Second, the project must be approachable through recognized communications knowledge and techniques. Third, the project must be feasible within the time limits of the course" (Wallace, 1988, p. 36).

"Using projects as part of the content of such a course offers several advantages. First, this format provides for close contact with faculty . . . It provides practical career-related experiences . . . [and] offer[s] the student a sense of accomplishment as they serve . . . in a quasi-professional, practical capacity" (Wallace, 1988, p. 35). Specifically, as a client project, it is a collaborative effort at problem solving; it develops interpersonal skills and uses evidence as a support for plans and decisions. Additionally, the concept of deadlines, persuasive argument, and personal responsibility are developed. Certainly, the project assists in establishing better corporate or institutional relationships and possibly creates partnerships among a school's various departments.

The project demonstrates the level of achievement reached by the student in communication and production skills. It also, as an experiential project, requires the student to interact on a close, personal, and regular basis with a client. The integration of this internship-type experience is a key element in helping the student learn contextual and adaptive competence and in developing a professional identity (Moore, 1987).

## The Oral Defense or Presentation

The content of this performance is based on the integration of the thesis and the project. It is a defense-presentation of the research study; it allows for a summarization of the literature review, discussion of its procedures, data, and recommendations. It also can review the project, exhibit the production or performance, and discuss its results applicable as a solution to the problem. As a public performance, oral and nonverbal expression can also be assessed.

## The Portfolio

A formal collection of works, which covers the full collegiate career of the student, the portfolio provides the evidence, documentation, and best samples of various types of creative expression and skills learning. Options exist for this portfolio to be submitted as evidence of learning or as a tool to be used in an employment search. In either case, the portfolio should show that specific aims of the curriculum have been mastered (see chapter 20).

## APPLIED RESEARCH

The senior thesis and accompanying project require the student to engage in intellectually productive research for a client. Typically referred to as applied communications research, the goal of the work is to solve problems and bring about change (Moore, 1988). O'Hair, Kreps, and Frey (1990) listed the various characteristics of a definition of applied research. Generally, applied research is the practical design of a workable solution for a real-world problem designed specifically for a particular client.

Using the terminology for the stages of applied research as identified by O'Hair and Kreps (1990), Table 21.3 lists and relates them to the cap-

TABLE 21.3
The Applied Research Model for the Senior Thesis and Project[a]

| Research Activities | Course Application |
| --- | --- |
| Problem Identification | Client interviews, project selection, research question, and analysis. |
| Conceptualization | Literature search: informal and institutional sources, library and database sources, interviews. |
| Operationalization | Transform the research findings into concrete approaches to solving the problem. Selecting project strategies based on evidence, credibility, and audience. |
| Measurement | Preproduction strategies, data gathering, observations, interviews relevant to the production of the project. |
| Analysis | Project production. Analysis of techniques, approaches, results of the project. |
| Recommendations | Discuss the ways in which the solution solved the problem: successes, weaknesses, suggested revisions. |

[a]Adapted from O'Hair and Kreps, 1990, p. 25.

TABLE 21.4
Outcomes Instruments as Related to Learning Modalities

| Instrument | Cognitive Learning | Affective Learning | Psychomotor Learning |
|---|---|---|---|
| Senior Thesis | X | X | |
| Senior Project | X | X | X |
| Oral Presentation | X | X | X |
| Portfolio | X | X | X |

stone course requirements, which incorporates the senior thesis and the accompanying senior project. The course requirements follow the systematic development of the research and literature review and integrates them with the project as a workable solution to a problem. Finally, and perhaps most importantly, it specifies as a final stage the process of evaluation of the solution.

Each of the course requirements, or learning measurement instruments, provides for individual differences in learning and permits demonstrated achievement in areas in which the student excels. In Table 21.4, each instrument is related to the specific type of learning modality applicable to it.

These course requirements enable the student to address and demonstrate achievement of the various outcomes statements, goal of the course, and skills expected of graduates of the curriculum by the institution. Table 21.5 summarizes and integrates those various aims of education within applicable learning styles and course requirements. (The course syllabus referred to here can be found on the author's homepage under Research, Capstone Course, at http://users.etown.edu/m/moorerc/).

## ASSESSING STUDENT PERFORMANCE

The capstone course is a learning experience that has the ability to draw together many diverse elements of prior learning to help determine if the academic goals and objectives of the institution and the department have been achieved. As a direct measure of student accomplishment of them, the course requirements allow the faculty member to assess student learning and performance as having, at least satisfactorily, met those expected outcomes.

The capstone course at Elizabethtown College uses the "Aims" noted in Table 21.5 as a basis for evaluating student performance in each of the course requirements. They have been translated into a student grad-

TABLE 21.5
Aims Achieved by the Evaluation Instruments

|  | Thesis | Project | Presentation | Portfolio |
|---|---|---|---|---|
| Cognitive Learning | Scholarly concern for advancing the profession through research.<br>Improve one's knowledge of the profession or discipline.<br>Ability to acquire, develop, convey, and integrate knowledge and information.<br>Critically examine issues.<br>Quantitative and qualitative analysis.<br>Evaluation of data collected and conclusions related to issues of thesis. | Advancing the professional through applied research.<br>Adaptive competence in relating knowledge to a project.<br>Discrimination between concepts applying relevant approaches to the problem.<br>Creative thinking and design of solutions: organization, treatment, production.<br>Leadership capacity to initiate, manage, and carry a project to conclusion. | Understanding of the communication or presentation process: informative, narrative persuasive, etc.<br>Use of supporting strategies and information: nonverbal communication, imagery, visual support, ethos-pathos, questioning, presentation of proof or reinforcement.<br>Strategy for organization: comparison and contrast, problem solving, etc.<br>Understanding the audience, shaping of ideas appropriately. | Works exhibit a broad range of abilities.<br>Shows imagination, concept development.<br>Shows an understanding of the responsibilities and attributes of a communicator. |

| | | | |
|---|---|---|---|
| Affective Learning | Understand the societal context of learning. Convey professional values and ethics. Show motivation for continued learning. | Applying knowledge, skills, values of profession or discipline to a new or unique problem. Assume a professional identity and exhibit professional responsibilities. Shows aesthetic sensibility. | Assumption of a proper professional identity appropriate for delivery of the thesis or project. Display an attitude for performance that indicates mastery of verbal techniques: clarity, relevance, effectiveness. Creative planning and presentation of thesis or project. | Professional value and interest is evident in preparation of the work. Presentation of work represents a professional identity. Creative approach to the display of work. |
| Psycho-motor Learning | Competence in reading, writing, research. Computer Literacy. Library Competency. | Mastering the skills of the profession and application of them to a project. Design, writing scripting, visual representation and production. | Performance Skills: nonverbal communication, oral communication skills, mediated presentation. Presentation skills and organization. Production and use of supporting materials. | Collection of mastered skills and abilities. Technical acumen evident in displayed work. |

ing-evaluation guideline that sets levels of performance for the student to be "satisfactory" or better in his or her demonstrated performance.

This rubric is a commentary about the standards for grading. It then lays out expectations for how student performance will be evaluated in each of the course requirements. This guide is shared with students early in the semester, reviewed often, and specifically referred to when the instructor provides evaluative comments on the thesis, project, and oral defense. Additionally, the elements of Table 21.5 are referred to in comments made during evaluation. Students are expected to continually refer to this grading-evaluation guideline so that they are also able to make a self-assessment of the work prior to submission or performance. Students who are graded "satisfactory" or higher on each of the course assessment instruments are judged to have met the minimum expectations of the department mission and course goal and objectives. (The standards and expectations referred to here can be found on the author's homepage under Research, Capstone Course, at http://users. etown.edu/m/moorerc/).

## ADVANTAGES OF THE CAPSTONE COURSE

The position presented in this chapter, and the examples provided, have focused on the integration of writing, speaking, and communicating through media. The chapter has also incorporated the need for a sense of aesthetics, creative expression, and experiential learning. The nature of differing curriculums in communications, especially those without a professional focus, requires the flexible application or alteration of capstone course requirements as necessary for the assessment provided by the course to be faithful to the specific mission statements of that department and institution.

The following list of advantages and characteristics of a capstone course are a summary of the educative value of such an experience for students presented in this chapter.

The capstone course . . .

- allows for the adaptation and integration of institutional mission statements, departmental or school mission statements, and course objectives to the general goals of higher education.
- can be a broad-based course drawing together disciplines across the university. This allows for unique partnerships to develop between departments resulting in a greater integration of them in the university fabric.
- allows conclusions to be drawn from student performance regarding the level of involvement in the liberal arts versus professional

training. It also enables faculty to address perceived weaknesses in a curriculum. Ongoing assessment in the capstone course allows for continual evaluation and development of the curriculum so that students are demonstrating that they are learning what faculty thinks they are teaching.

- can address and incorporate new approaches and objectives, as curricula and expectations change or expand.
- can be tailored to measure outcomes in any of the various divisions or configurations of the communications field. Research projects can be applied to a wide variety of interests, issues, or professional settings.
- places expectations on students so that they become independent learners. The course is student-centered and self-directed, allowing each student to work at a pace with which he or she is most comfortable and in a direction suitable to career aspirations.
- requires students to perform at higher level of learning by requiring them to engage in analysis, synthesis, and evaluation of past learning and apply it to new experiences. "Faculty report that . . . research . . . [is] the most effective method to teach [such] critical thinking" (Lockhart & Borland, 2001, p. 19).
- as a summative tool, provides the opportunity to evaluate students at the end of their major program of study and at the end of their collegiate career.
- is a multifaceted method of assessment. It goes beyond examinations and simple projects by integrating various assessment strategies. These, particularly, include a senior thesis, an applied project drawn from the thesis, a public oral defense-performance, and a portfolio.
- allows students to perform and excel in those learning modalities most appropriate to him or her.
- integrates skill demonstrations into objectives of an experiential nature, providing a real opportunity for business and industry alliances.

## DISADVANTAGES OF THE CAPSTONE COURSE

Although one generally might not argue against the evaluation of learning or against the summative evaluation of the entire learning experience, capstone course experiences do have several limitations. As such, the departmental faculty needs to clearly be satisfied that this level and type of assessment is adequate from which to draw conclusions about student achievement and the curriculum.

The capstone course . . .

- evaluates students' knowledge, identity and skills subjectively.
- may allow less motivated and goal oriented students too much flexibility by focusing on independent and self-directed learning.
- can be too unfocused unless the faculty monitors departmental curricular expectations as they evolve and adjust the course.
- requires faculty to depart from self-serving or specialized agenda and focus on an integrated experience where the "compleat" communicator is more important than the specialist.
- places a great demand on student time, learning, and performance. Many students may not be up to the task.
- may allow a student to excel in a favored learning modality but does not easily assist students who perform in an average way, or below, in other modalities. There is typically no course of remediation for problems and failures.
- allows a student to approach the goal of curricular integration but does not always specify to what level that occurs. It does not specify how various levels of success can be quantified and translated into a summary of positive performance of attaining the curriculum's mission.

All four instruments (thesis, project, defense or presentation, and portfolio) of evaluation are strengths in the course. They draw their success from their variety of approaches and the way in which each of the course requirements integrate with each other to create a complete picture of student achievement. Yet, that variety and sheer workload are very demanding in terms of faculty and student commitment and time. Although tempting to make the course less time consuming, elimination of any one of the instruments weakens the course because each in isolation cannot be the summative tool of assessment that they are when integrated. Any one of the instruments does not allow for written, oral, and mediated expression in all three modalities of learning.

A survey of a variety of types of capstone courses was conducted by Henscheid (2000). The study reviews structure, goal, objectives, requirements, operation, and many other aspects of various capstone courses.

## CONCLUSION

Communications programs have evolved greatly in the last century. Having originated from programs like English, curriculums gradually became more specialized and moved further away from the core program of the university. In the more recent past, the field became fragmented and more vocational (Rowland, 1991). Today, the debate has brought us back to our roots, to the liberal arts. The "new professionalism" positions the communications curriculum at the center of the university program. Driven by intellectual pursuit, the program espouses integration of learning, linkages between departments, and, perhaps most importantly, the elevation of the message to all-important status.

The diverse fields that make up the discipline of communication are blending. Yet, the one unchanging element in the mix is the message:

> Creation of the message, regardless of the medium, always has been at the core of communication education. This is a distinction that critics of the discipline have long failed to understand: What is most central to our curriculum is not the how of communicating messages—what buttons to push or writing or speaking style to affect—but the what of message content. (Pease, 1994, p. 9)

Such is the focus and the value of the capstone course. The capstone course is the curricular embodiment of convergence. The course is the single opportunity for all of the knowledge and skills to be drawn together. The course ties knowledge and experience together, from the totality of the student educational experience requiring a critical assessment and unique application of 4 years of learning to the successful completion of course requirements. Drawn into the mix are the course expectations that university core courses, and those from any configuration of courses selected, will be drawn on to demonstrate a command of knowledge and ability. The course defines a basic education, a basic expectation; it outlines a level of academic and professional performance that fosters criticism and creativity. The capstone course draws together the expected outcomes of higher education, the institution, and the department, into one educational experience so that those who graduate have shown that they possess more than a sheepskin. They are ". . . well-informed, inquisitive, open-minded young people who are both productive and reflective, seeking answers to life's most important questions . . . who not only pursue their own personal interests but are also prepared to fulfill their social and civic obligations" ("Prologue and Major Recommendations," 1986, p. 16).

## REFERENCES

Accrediting Council on Education in Journalism and Mass Communication. (2003). *Accrediting standards*. Retrieved December 18, 2003, from http://www.ukans.edu/~acejmc/BREAKING/New_standards_9-03.pdf

American Association of Higher Education. (n.d.). *9 principles of good practice for assessing student learning*. Retrieved January 2, 2004, from http://www.aahe.org/assessment/principl.htm

Andreasen, R. J., & Trede, L. D. (1998, December). *A comparison of the perceived benefits of selected activities between capstone and non-capstone courses in a college of agriculture*. Paper presented at the meeting of the American Vocational Association, New Orleans, LA.

Association of American Colleges. (n.d.). *A search for quality and coherence in baccalaureate education* (project on redefining the meaning and purpose of baccalaureate degrees). Washington, DC: Author.

Blanchard, R. O., & Christ, W. G. (1993). *Media education and the liberal arts*. Hillsdale, NJ: Lawrence Erlbaum Associates, Inc.

Bloom, B. S. (1956). *A taxonomy of educational objectives: Handbook I, the cognitive domain*. New York: Longman.

Bloom, B. S. (1971). Affective consequences of school achievement. In J. H. Block (Ed.), *Mastery learning* (pp. 13–28). New York: Holt, Rinehart & Winston.

Boyer, E. L. (1987). *College: The undergraduate experience in America*. New York: Harper & Row.

Carlson, C. D., & Peterson, R. J. (1993). Social problems and policy: A capstone course. *Teaching Sociology, 21,* 239–241.

Cuseo, J. B. (1998). Objectives and benefits of senior year programs. In J. N. Gardner & G. Van der Veer (Eds.), *The senior year experience: Facilitating integration, reflection, closure, and transition* (pp. 21–36). San Francisco: Jossey-Bass.

Glaser, H. F., & Radliff, A. J. (2000). *Integrating service learning into the communication capstone course*. Unpublished manuscript, University of Nebraska at Omaha. (ERIC Document Reproduction Service No. ED 444199)

Henscheid, J. M. (2000). *Professing the disciplines: An analysis of senior seminars and capstone courses* (The First-Year Monograph Series No. 30). Columbia, SC: The National Research Center for the Freshman Year Experience and Students in Transition. (ERIC Document Reproduction Service No. ED 446711)

Kemp, J. E. (1975). *Planning and producing audiovisual materials* (3rd ed.). New York: Crowell.

Kemp, J. E., & Smellie, D. C. (1989). *Planning, producing, and using instructional media* (6th ed.). New York: HarperCollins.

Kings College. (1986). *The growth of a model college*. Wilkes-Barre, PA: Author.

Levine, A. (1998). A president's personal and historical perspective. In J. N. Gardner & G. Van der Veer (Eds.), *The senior year experience: Facilitating integration, reflection, closure, and transition* (pp. 51–59). San Francisco: Jossey-Bass.

Lockhart, M., & Borland, Jr., K. W. (2001). Critical thinking goals, outcomes and pedagogy in senior capstone courses. *The Journal of Faculty Development, 18,* 19–26.

Moore, R. C. (1987, February). *A hierarchical program of experiential learning opportunities in communications education*. Paper presented at the meeting of the Association for Educational Communications and Technology, Atlanta, GA.

Moore, R. C. (1988, January). *The role of applied research in undergraduate communications education*. Paper presented at the meeting of the Association for Educational Communications and Technology, New Orleans, LA.

Murphy, P. D. (2003). *Capstone experience*. Retrieved January 3, 2004, from North Dakota State University Web site: http://www.ndsu.edu/ndsu/accreditation/assessment/capstone_experience.htm

Newton, J. (n.d.). *Research on capstone courses*. Retrieved January 5, 2004, from York University Web site: http://www.yorku.ca/jnewton/curriculum/capstone.htm

O'Hair, D., & Kreps, G. L. (1990). *Applied communication theory and research*. Hillsdale, NJ: Lawrence Erlbaum Associates, Inc.

O'Hair, D., Kreps, G. L., & Frey, L. R. (1990). Conceptual issues. In D. O'Hair & G. L. Kreps (Eds.), *Applied communication theory and research* (pp. 3–22). Hillsdale, NJ: Lawrence Erlbaum Associates, Inc.

Oliva, P. F. (1982). *Developing the curriculum*. Boston: Little, Brown.

Pease, E. C. (1994, Spring). Defining communication's role and identity in the 1990's: Promises and opportunities for journalism and communication studies. *Association of Schools of Journalism and Mass Communication Insights*, 13–17.

Prologue and major recommendations for Carnegie Foundations report on colleges. (1986, November 5). *The Chronicle of Higher Education, 33*, 16–22.

Redmond, M. V. (1998). Outcomes assessment and the capstone course in communication. *The Southern Communication Journal, 64*, 68–75.

Rowland, Jr., W. D. (1991, August). *The role of journalism and communications studies in the liberal arts: A place of honor*. Paper presented at the meeting of the Association for Education and Journalism in Mass Communication, Boston.

Smith, B. L. (1998). Curricular structures for cumulative learning. In J. N. Gardner & G. Van der Veer (Eds.), *The senior year experience: Facilitating integration, reflection, closure, and transition* (pp. 81–94). San Francisco: Jossey-Bass.

Smith, W. (1993). The capstone course at Loras College. *Teaching Sociology, 21*, 250–252.

Volkwein, J. F. (2003, May). *Implementing outcomes assessment on your campus. eJournal, 1*, Article 2. Retrieved January 5, 2004, from http://rpgroup.org/publications/eJournal/Volume_1/volkwein.htm

Wagenaar, T. C. (1993). The capstone course. *Teaching Sociology, 21*, 209–214.

Wallace, R. C. (1988). A capstone course in applied sociology. *Teaching Sociology, 16*, 34–40.